WOODBURNING:
ART & CRAFT

Also by the Author

Clay Craft at Home

WOODBURNING:
ART & CRAFT

Techniques, Designs,
Decorations, and Inspiration

BY ELAINE BROADWATER

Crown Publishers, Inc.,
New York

Inquiries should be addressed to Crown Publishers, Inc., One Park Avenue, New York, New York 10016

Printed in the United States of America

Published simultaneously in Canada by General Publishing Company Limited

Library of Congress Cataloging in Publication Data

Broadwater, Elaine.
    Woodburning, art and craft.

    Includes index.
    1. Pyrography. I. Title.
TT199.8.B76   1980   745.51   79–19408
ISBN: 0–517–535874 (cloth)
        0–517–535882 (paper)

Design by Deborah B. Kerner

10 9 8 7 6 5 4 3 2 1
First edition

CONTENTS

ACKNOWLEDGMENTS

A majority of the unfinished wooden products used in this book were furnished by Adco Redwood, Inc., Clauss Manufacturing, Corner Cupboard Crafts, Inc., O. P. Crafts, Co., Inc., Walnut Hollow, and Woodring Craft. Woodring Craft also loaned part of their woodburning collection for photography and also supplied some pictures.

The wood finishes were supplied by Deft and Illinois Bronze while General Crafts Corporation furnished the air drying modeling wood. Advice and encouragement from Post Electric Co. were helpful.

Some of the drawings and designs were created by Lisa Petranoff, and Regina Petrutis and Phillip Zeller were both cooperative in supplying pictures and information.

It is my pleasure to be able to acknowledge and publicly thank these people for their help. A special thanks must go to my husband, George Broadwater, for his finishing of each project, his photography, and his patience.

INTRODUCTION

The author of a novel has the opportunity to set the stage for his/her writing, and it seemed only fair that this writer of a craft instruction book be granted the same privilege. Really, in this case, these words are to quantify the title and explain my purpose in writing this book.

Woodburning through the ages has meant everything from using a firebrand or a blowtorch to scorching wood with primitive decorative designs up to contemporary pyrography where an electric woodburning pen is used. We will concentrate on woodburning with a pyrolectric pen and leave the other older techniques to others to explain.

Because of past experiences as a reader, I have always refused to write about any craft that I have not actually accomplished myself. Therefore, most of the projects in this book were designed and woodburned by me, and finished and photographed by my husband, George. The main exception to this is in the final chapter where three modern artists share their woodburning talents and photographs with us. All other exceptions are noted by the individual craftsperson's credit.

The possible progression of woodburning from a craft technique to an art medium is deliberate. Though I make no claim to be an artist in the typical definition of the term, the years have proved that teaching the novice crafter is more my talent. My guiding theory is that a craft is a creative pursuit where the participant follows someone else's designs and directions. Some of you may find that you belong in the same category as myself—an avid craftsperson who, though limited by lack of artistic talent, still enjoys creative satisfaction through the mastering of an easy craft technique, woodburning.

This same craft technique may become an art when some individuals after practice combine their own designs and procedures with a degree of God-given artistic talent to create an original work that resembles no other and possesses a beauty of its own.

This could have been just a picture book of fine art if the stress on the quality of art was our purpose. However, we were striving to encourage you to become involved in woodburning, and enjoy doing the craft yourself. To what degree you refine that talent is not as important to us as the degree of creative satisfaction you may gain by trying!

PART ONE

WOODBURNING
AS A CRAFT TECHNIQUE

1 BASIC SUPPLIES FOR WOODBURNING

In pyrography (woodburning with an electric pen), the main craft tool you will need is a *pyrolectric pen.* When is a craft tool sometimes not recognized in that capacity? When you look at it and think you recognize it as a toy that you used for fun years ago as a child. Many people's first exposure to woodburning was after receiving a woodburning pen as a Christmas gift. That very recognition and your memories of joyful accomplishment with it are part of the reasons why pyrography is one of the craft categories rapidly gaining popularity. It also accents the reason why I wrote this book, hoping to encourage you to move beyond the toy stage with your woodburning and to begin to enjoy the craft and art of pyrography. Woodburning can appeal to male and female alike and to a wide range of ages. When you have used the pyrolectric pen as a craft tool and have practiced your burn strokes a little, you will know that you are capable of using such a tool for more than just a toy.

Another major reason for woodburning's rapidly growing acceptance as a craft or art technique is the improved pyrolectric tool (which still answers to the name of woodburning pen). It can be used for many burning techniques on many practical home accessories or decorative projects, rather than just burning a stamped picture on a piece of very soft wood. One example of such an improved tool is the one I normally use, which is manufactured by Post Electric Co. (see drawing 1–1).

Unlike some woodburning pens that are designed as small soldering irons or toys, this pyrolectric pen was designed specifically to be used

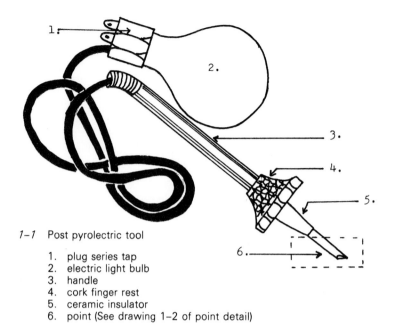

1–1   Post pyrolectric tool

1. plug series tap
2. electric light bulb
3. handle
4. cork finger rest
5. ceramic insulator
6. point (See drawing 1–2 of point detail)

as an art/craft tool. Of course, it can be used by children who are old enough to practice the safety precautions necessary for using any woodburning tool.

This pen is made with the point permanently fixed in position. The shape of the point, detailed in drawing 1–2, is such that changing to other sizes or shapes of points is not necessary, regardless of the material on which it is being used to burn on the design effect desired.

1–2   Pyrolectric woodburning pen point detail
1. heel
2. edge
3. tip
4. flat plane
5. rod

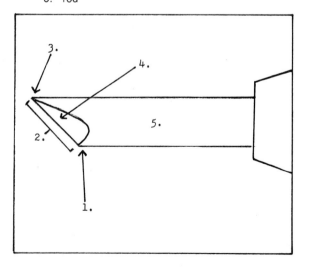

Permanent placement of the point protects the fine heating element that is in it and provides durability. The very fineness of this heating element requires the use of resistance, which is conveniently provided by an electric light bulb in the plug series tap (see drawing 1–1). This feature, unique to this pen, maintains a uniform degree of heat in the point, enabling the artist or craftsperson to control the burning effect more accurately, and it can be used on different types of materials, such as leather, paper, cork, and so on, as well as on woods of different hardness. The temperature of the point may be raised or lowered by changing the light bulb to a higher or lower wattage. The pen can be plugged into any normal 110-volt household current.

You can use a bulb of lower wattage in the plug series tap when burning on velvet, other cloths and papers, heavy cardboard, balsam, and very soft woods. A 75–100-watt bulb, while burning leather and softwoods, and a 100–125-watt bulb for harder woods will do the trick for you. Do not use a bulb higher than 125 watts in the plug series tap.

Precaution: Choose a light bulb of the correct wattage for the material of your project if you are using the Post pyrolectric pen. Screw it into the plug series tap of the pen and *then* insert the tap into a wall plug. *Do not touch the point or any part of the light bulb while the tool is plugged into electricity or while it is still hot!* Have an asbestos board or some other nonflammable material on which to rest the pen when you lay it down. *Never leave a pen plugged into electricity when leaving a room or near unattended small children.* Using this electrical tool is no more dangerous than using any other electrical tool, but it does require using common sense and normal safety precautions.

Though the Post pyrolectric pen is mentioned often here, I do not mean to indicate that other brands of pens cannot be as useful. Several companies have improved their pens in recent years. See the names of some in Supply Sources in the back of the book. Besides the use of the plug series tap, these other pens generally differ from the Post pen in that additional overpoints can be screwed onto the pen over the original point. Usually I do not use the overpoints, preferring to obtain the numerable burning effects by using various positions of the original point. You can practice these techniques, detailed in this book, and achieve them quite well with either type of woodburning pen. Or you can elect to use the overpoints. Experience will teach you which method works best for you.

The modern versatility of the woodburning pen means you can use it now in ways you may not have thought possible. Personalized designs can be achieved on all types of wood, including weathered and unfinished plaques, wooden rings, frames, poles, and furniture. A different type of "country carved" look can be created by burning the lines instead of carving them. Then add decorative paint colors. The burned design lines not only are a beautiful brown color, but they also seal the wood and prevent paint seepage and provide accent. Lightly burned strokes can be combined into many different ethnic designs. But you will see and read about such examples in this book. Let's get back to what other supplies you will need to woodburn.

Often a beginning woodburner does not have even *sanding supplies* available while woodburning because he/she forgets these three important steps.

1. Presanding the wooden object, before starting to burn it, is required. If you have purchased from a craft supply shop the wooden objects that are presanded and ready for finishing, you will not need to sand as long or use as coarse a sandpaper as though you had bought it off the lumberyard shelves. Usually the medium Sandrite® sanding pad or #200–400 sandpaper will be satisfactory for this preliminary sanding.

2. Rubbing the woodburned design lightly with a fine sanding pad or #600 sandpaper *after* burning is important to do before finishing. You will use the same sanding supplies in the next step.

3. After the application of two coats of finish to your project and an appropriate drying time, your project should be rubbed firmly with the fine sanding pad or #600 (very fine) sandpaper before the final coats of finish. Some decoupeurs use #0000 (very fine) steel wool for this task.

You will also need a piece of #200 sandpaper or a pad of coarse steel wool on which you can clean the pen point, though that is really not sanding, is it?

Mention has been made of sanding pads, and you may not be familiar with them. You can purchase sanding and finishing pads in many craft or paint supply stores. They are man-made abrasive pads (one brand is called Sandrite®) that seldom produce scratch marks, though they will sand well. You can use either side of a pad or it can be wrapped around a sanding block, used alone, or doubled without cracking. It does not feel gritty on the hands. Each time you use one, you can wash the sanding dust out of it, let it dry, and use it over and over again.

Tracing and drawing supplies include many things you probably already have around the house—a pencil, large eraser, metal edge ruler, compass, and tracing paper. If you are tracing patterns on wood, use graphite tracing paper, rather than the usual carbon, as it is less apt to smudge and cause spots that will be difficult to remove.

Finishing supplies are an absolute must in my estimation because practically any woodburned project gains beauty with the proper wood finish. First, what brand of wood finish is best? Who really knows? Most artists, craftspeople, and retailers would simply recommend their own favorites and I am no different. However, many brands will perform satisfactorily for you. If one brand is not available locally, take the advice of your craft supply retailer when he suggests another.

After testing and trying many brands and kinds of wood finish, we finally settled on a fast-drying, clear, lacquer-type finish such as Deft for brushing and Illinois Bronze decoupage finish for spraying. The manufacturer usually suggests on the label what type of applicator works best with that finish. Choose your finish and then buy the appropriate brush. You will find more information about finishing in chapter 2.

Secondly, do not forget to buy some finish thinner and/or brush cleaner. Some wood finishes require a special thinner and brush cleaner, especially the lacquer type.

Why have we not suggested using the gluelike, water-base finishes that are so popular for "quicky" craft use? Primarily because some water-base finishes may raise the grain of the wood excessively, may not tone the wood, and may not give the depth of finish that a woodburning craftsperson desires. Some may even cause certain woods to have a whitish, gray, or greenish cast that is not particularly attractive with a warm brown, woodburned design.

Acrylic paints were also used during the production of some of the projects for this book. Why use acrylics and not oils? Because they dry quickly and are compatible with the wood finish we used. If you use oil paints in combination with your woodburning, you must use a compatible wood finish over it to avoid the possibility of crackling and peeling.

Protective supplies, such as asbestos board or other nonflammable metal tray or pan (to lay the woodburning pen on when it is not being used), are needed. The other protective supplies that some woodburners advise are not absolutely necessary, such as asbestos glove, tongs, and asbestos pad to lay under the project while you are burning it. The best protection against an accidental burn from the pen is to keep your mind on your work and use common sense. The pen point will be hot and will burn if you touch it—so don't!

In most of your projects you will be burning on wood, so let's talk about the kinds of wood that you may be using.

Woods differ in grain, figure, texture, hardness, color, and other physical characteristics. If we wanted to really get involved in the study of woods, we could spend a lot of time discovering how different trees grow, the difference in wood formations and cell structures, and so on. We could learn how lumber is cut and how to identify many different species. (Two good reference books on this subject are *What Wood Is That* by Herbert Edlin, Viking Press, and *Know Your Woods* by Albert Constantine, Jr., Scribner's.)

What we need to know now is how different unfinished woods will respond to woodburning, finishing, and the general appearance of the finished project. You will note that information about hardness, grain, figure, color, and texture of the different woods that you may use for woodburning are listed here. Let's pause for just a few words of explanation about the terms being used before you examine the list.

Hardness: All woods are said to be hard or soft to one degree or another. Softwoods are usually from coniferous or needle-leaved trees. The formation and composition of the cells within the tree make the difference. You may note a little oozing of resin or a slight turpentine smell when you burn on a softwood. You will not want to apply as much pressure on the pen, and it will burn faster than a hardwood does. It also does not require as hot a pen to burn as do the hardwoods.

Hardwoods are from broad-leaved trees (with a few exceptions like poplars). These hardwood trees are usually grown where there are two distinct growing seasons each year, such as a hot and cold season or a wet and dry season. In all these trees, the wood formed in one season (springwood) differs from the wood cells that are grown in another season such as summer (summerwood). Springwood is normally lighter in color and weight and only moderately strong, as compared to summerwood, which is usually heavier, darker, and stronger. This pair of wood layers, produced each season, makes up the annual ring and, with the characteristics of the pores, strongly influences the "figure" of the cut wood.

Grain: The terms "grain" and "figure" are often interchangeable but, strictly speaking, grain means the direction of the fibrous elements of the wood cells. (This is important for you to know as you are told to sand *with* the grain. Also the grain can cause the woodburning pen point to deviate from its intended path unless you apply more pressure and burn slower on the grain.)

A specific piece of cut unfinished wood may have either a (1) straight, (2) diagonal, (3) spiral, (4) interlocked, or (5) wavy grain. This has been influenced by the way the wood was cut, as well as how the tree grew. We will qualify the grain for our purposes as distinct, faint, or invisible. If it is not invisible, you can visually determine the direction of the grain. When a wood has a distinct grain, i.e., you will find burning *with* the grain or straight *across* the grain easier than to burn on a diagonal to that grain. With practice, you will master burning on any grain.

Figure: This is the natural design, or pattern, that you can see on the cut surface of the wood. Not only the type of grain, but also the growth rings (annual rings of springwood and summerwood), vascular rays, variations in color, method of cutting, presence of burls, and knots and crotches in that particular piece of wood combine to result in a visible figure. There are so many names for different types of figures, and a majority are commercially inspired so we are not concerned with classification. The figure present on the wood should always be taken into consideration when you are planning your woodburned design. We will talk more about the use of figure in chapter 5 when we explore the possibilities of making use of the wood's dimension, grain, and figure in planning woodburned designs.

Texture: If you have ever rubbed your hand lightly over different kinds of unfinished wood, there is a texture on the surface of that wood that feels either coarse or fine, even or uneven. This factor of texture results from the width and abundance of vascular rays and the dimensions of the pores or cells in the wood, as well as how it was cut.

Ring-porous wood, with marked differences between springwood and summerwood, is apt to be an uneven, coarse texture. (As a beginning woodburner, avoid using very fine or intricate designs on uneven, coarse-textured wood.) Vice versa, wood that is diffuse porous and shows little difference between springwood and summerwood usually has an even, fine texture and makes the burning of small intricate designs on it easier. (Of course, there are exceptions.) Softwoods are more apt to be fine or moderately coarse-textured. With some textures it may mean that you will have to compensate when burning it—going slower on the harder summerwood, faster and with a lighter touch on the softer springwood to create an even burn overall.

Color: The color of different unfinished woods is fairly obvious to the eye. Some woods also possess the ability to reflect light from their cell walls and have a resultant definite luster that is very attractive. The lack of such a luster on wood that is a whitish color is sometimes reason enough to stain or paint that particular piece of wood, as well as using a woodburned design. (Remember that wood finish application will almost always darken any wood slightly, without a stain. Some water-base finishes may bring a gray or greenish cast to white woods.) However, woodburning should be mainly used to enhance the natural beauty of a wooden project, so do not always hide a beautiful figure, grain, luster, or color if it is present. As a rule, it was our practice to use a clear wood finish (fast-drying, lacquer-type) on all the projects in this book. If additional stain or paints were used, these will be indicated in the instructions.

List of woods commonly used for woodburning projects
(a) Hardness (b) Grain (c) Figure (d) Color (e) Texture
**Especially recommended for beginners

Alderwood**
 a) moderately hard, resembles cherry
 b) faint grain
 c) subtle, attractive figure
 d) light brown, tinged with red
 e) even, fine texture

Ash
 a) hard
 b) distinct grain
 c) strong figure pattern
 d) whitish color
 e) uneven, coarse texture

Aspen Poplar
- a) soft
- b) obscure grain
- c) very little obvious figure
- d) very pale yellow
- e) uneven texture

Basswood**
- a) moderately hard (called "soft" by some authors)
- b) faint grain
- c) subtle figure
- d) creamy white
- e) even, fine texture

Beech
- a) hard
- b) faint grain
- c) lacks obvious figure
- d) small flecks of dark brown on pinkish brown
- e) even texture

Birch
- a) hard
- b) faint grain
- c) very little figure unless cut specially
- d) pale brownish yellow
- e) even, fine texture

Boxwood
- a) hard
- b) straight grain
- c) subtle figure unless specially cut
- d) yellowish white
- e) even, fine texture

Cherry
- a) hard
- b) distinct grain
- c) dappled figure
- d) golden brown with hint of green
- e) even texture

Douglas Fir
- a) soft
- b) distinct grain
- c) obvious figure
- d) red brown summerwood and yellowish pink springwood
- e) uneven texture

Elm
- a) soft
- b) distinct wavy grain
- c) obvious figure, sometimes called "partridge breast"
- d) warm brown
- e) uneven texture with interlocked grain

Mahogany
- a) soft
- b) faint grain, closely knit and even
- c) attractive figure as rays reflect light
- d) coppery red, fades under strong sunlight, darkens under moderate light
- e) even, fine texture

Maple
- a) hard (sycamore maple is softer)
- b) distinct but subdued grain
- c) attractive figure
- d) yellowish white with darker biscuit brown summerwood, has attractive luster
- e) even, fine texture

Oak
- a) hard
- b) distinct grain
- c) very obvious figure
- d) yellowish brown, may appear to be two colors because of pale rays
- e) uneven, coarse texture

Pine
- a) soft
- b) distinct grain
- c) obvious figure
- d) reddish brown summerwood, yellow springwood
- e) even and moderately coarse texture

Redwood
- a) moderately hard
- b) obvious grain
- c) distinct figure
- d) reddish brown
- e) moderately coarse texture

Walnut**
- a) hard
- b) faint grain
- d) dark brown
- e) moderately coarse but uniform texture

Western Red Cedar
- a) soft to moderately hard
- b) faint grain
- c) subtle figure
- d) reddish brown, weathers to silvery gray
- e) even, fine texture

2 BASIC PROCEDURES AND BURN STROKES

Please read this entire chapter carefully before you start to actually woodburn. Even if you have woodburned before and are anxious to start on one of the projects, there might be something a little different about our techniques and procedures. This is an outline of the basic procedures.

I. Select and prepare the surface on which you are going to burn.

A. Beginners should start by using unfinished, seasoned wood. It is handy if it has been presanded as the pieces are that can be purchased in craft supply shops. Avoid using wood that has already been stained or treated with an oil-base product. It is possible to design-burn through *acrylic* paint or wood stain, but you must clean your pen point more often and your burned lines are not apt to be as fine or even as you would like.

It pays to *know the specific characteristics of the wooden piece* you are going to burn to ensure ease of woodburning and complete satisfaction with the finished piece. Is it hard or soft wood? You will need a hotter point to burn the harder wood. Does it have a subdued, even grain or a "wild" wide figure? It is discouraging to try to burn a fine, intricate design on a strongly patterned wood unless you are prepared to compensate. Will the color of the wood stay the same, darken slightly or a lot, or turn gray or white when the final finish is applied at the end of

Burn thru, acrylic Pain stain

12

the procedure? (Note again the list of woods and their characteristics in chapter 1.)

The characteristics of your particular piece of wood will also play an important role in your choice of a design to burn on it. It may have an interesting grain that should be incorporated into the design. (See the information about making use of the wood's dimension, grain, and figure in chapter 5.) If it is a soft, wild-figure wood, you will be happier using a bold, simple design that will not be overcome by the natural pattern of the wood. Sometimes you may want to paint or stain sections of the design, or the background around it, to subdue the grain.

Any sanding, repair, or carpentry that must be done on the wood should be completed before you start burning. A decoupage teacher once told me that many finished decoupage projects just miss being really fine examples because the basic sanding was not done before the decoupage process was started. That same principle is true when wood-burning. Most of the wooden plaques, boxes, frames, rings, and so on that you purchase unfinished in a craft supply shop have been pre-sanded so they will require only a light shading with fine sandpaper and a thorough wiping with a soft, clean cloth to remove fine particles and dust.

B. *Select and apply design to wood surface.* Here you have lots of choices, not only in designs but also in methods of application. A geometric design can usually be measured and drawn lightly with a lead pencil right on the wood. Do not press hard enough to indent the wood. If you use a light touch, mistakes, or "mind changes," can be erased with no trouble.

A design may also be traced onto the surface. Use graphite tracing paper rather than ordinary carbon to avoid smudges that might be hard to remove by erasing or sanding. Personally, since I cannot draw as well as I would like, I prefer to trace the main outline of a design on the wood and then attempt to pencil sketch in the remainder of the lines when necessary. After you have practiced and gained more confidence, you will find yourself more and more drawing your design directly on the wood or just marking some reference points with a pencil and burning "freehand."

II. Prepare your pyrolectric pen with a bulb of the proper voltage and your worktable. Your worktable should be the right height so you can comfortably sit at it and reach the wooden piece easily. There should be an asbestos pad or board (or some other nonflammable material such as metal) placed at one side of the work space, where you can conveniently lay the hot woodburning pen when need be. A metal pie tin or loaf pan will serve if you are leery of having asbestos around the house. Be sure the pan is large enough so that the pen will stay in it securely. You do not want to ever try to catch a hot woodburning pen as it falls to the floor or onto the tabletop!

Another necessary precaution is to have the cord leading from your pen to the electrical socket protected or laid aside so that no one can possibly trip over it and pull the pen from your hands. *Never touch the point or any part of the light bulb in the plug series tap while the tool is plugged in or while it is still hot! Never leave a plugged in woodburning tool unattended in a room where there are children or others not aware of the possibility of burning themselves!*

These precautions are emphasized because some people still look at a woodburning pen as a traditional toy and fail to use "common sense" caution. In all the years that I have been woodburning, I have never been burned simply because I acknowledge the fact that a burn is possible and always use the pen as I would any other electrical tool—with caution.

Keep a pad of fine steel wool or a piece of #200 sandpaper in your metal holding pan or on the asbestos board. You will need to wipe the point of your pen on this pad at regular intervals while you are burning. This cleans the carbon from the point that naturally accumulates while you are burning. *Do not touch the hot point with your fingers!* (If you use a pen with interchangeable points, keep a pliers and heat-proof gloves nearby to handle the points and do not try to change them when the pen is still very hot.) It is helpful to have a scrap of wood handy to test the temperature of the point on when you start burning or to practice strokes. Sometimes you can use the back of your wooden piece for this purpose—if it will not show when your project is finished.

Plug your pyrolectric pen into the electrical outlet and wait three to five minutes for it to attain the proper temperature. *Burn your design* into the wood piece using the basic burn strokes described in this chapter. Later, with practice, you will develop variations of these strokes for yourself. Remember to have a pretty clear idea of your design in your head and on the wood, or a sketch before you start burning. Once a line is burned, it is permanent! Erase any remaining pencil marks.

2–1   Hold the pyrolectric pen in your hand as though it were a large strong pencil or pen. Do not use more pressure than in using a strong pencil, as the depth of the burning does not depend upon the pressure exerted, but upon the length of time the pen point is allowed to burn and upon the position of the pen.

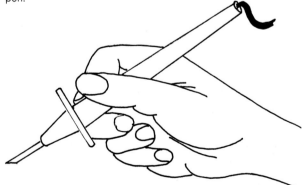

III. Finish your project.

A. When you have completed all your burning, *rub the entire surface with a fine finishing pad* or #600 sandpaper. This will remove some of the ragged edges of the burning, also any unerased pencil marks or excess carbon residue. It tends to smooth the surface without disturbing the burned design. Wipe the project thoroughly with a clean, dry, soft cloth. If particles of carbon or dust lodge in indentations, brush them out with a clean, soft bristle paintbrush.

B. Now is the time to use acrylic paint, wood stains, or transparent oils, if you intend to use them at all on this particular project. (Do not fall into the habit of *always* adding these features to your woodburned projects as there is a lot of natural beauty in just the tones of the wood and the burned design alone.) The burned lines have a tendency to restrain the stain or paint within them and do not allow the paint to seep beyond the area in which you place them.

Try to avoid painting or staining right over your burned design lines because it dulls the rich brown color. You will read more about different ways to combine woodburning designs with painted accents and stains in the instructions for projects in this book.

Spray-seal acrylic paints or stains with acrylic sealer to avoid any bleeding of the color when you apply the final finish. Be sure your wood finish is compatible if you use oils for color, rather than acrylics.

C. The crowning touch on a woodburned project is the *final finish*. Too many woodburners skip this step. Unless you are striving to achieve a very rustic, subdued design or are working on a weathered or oiled wood, you will want to use this final finish step. It protects the wood and the design, as well as enriching the varied shades of brown caused by the burned design lines.

Apply two coats of clear, fast-drying, decoupage-type wood finish over the project by spraying, brushing, or dipping it. Which method is best? It depends upon your preference and how thick a finish you want, as well as upon certain facts about the project itself. (One brush coat equals approximately three to four thin spray coats. One dip coat equals about two to three brush coats.)

Sometimes the dimensions and shape of the project will make the determination for you. Some things are too large to dip, some are too small to conveniently spray or brush. Some have intricate areas that require spraying to enable you to reach those areas. Brush coats are the most economical. Dip coats will produce the thickest coating the fastest. Use a gloss finish if you want the final result to be shiny. Mix the finish well before starting the application and *always work in a well-ventilated room* where the temperature is approximately 70°.

1. Are you familiar with the *brush application* of this type of fast-drying finish? I use a nylon bristle brush that will allow easy flow of the

finish from the bristles to the surface of the project. Use the size brush that is appropriate for the size of the area to be coated. Dip the brush into the finish and let the excess drip back into the can. (Do not wipe the brush against the edge of the can because you can pick up bits of dried finish or other material on your brush.) *Flow* the finish onto the surface and don't try to "scrub" or overbrush back over the applied finish as it tends to dry very rapidly from the top down. The first coat will actually soak into the wood to some degree and will appear to be dry in minutes. Avoid overlapping strokes as much as possible. If you must smooth out a rough area, a puddle, or a drip of finish use a finish-moistened brush to lightly stroke it away—not a dry brush.

After the appropriate drying time (check the label for the manufacturer's recommendations), turn the project around one-quarter turn. This enables you to brush the second coat across the strokes of the first coat so that you will now coat any areas that you might have missed in the first coat.

When the second coat is thoroughly dry (perhaps I am overcautious, but I like to let it dry overnight), rub the entire surface with a fine finishing pad. Wipe off the dust and apply two more coats of the finish (with drying time between coats, of course).

If you desire a deeper depth to your finish, just continue applying coats of finish. Remember to rub down the project with a fine finishing pad between every two coats.

2. If you are using a *spray application,* remember to spray correctly. Shake the aerosol can of finish to be sure the contents are well mixed. Lay the project on newspapers (or place in a spray box) in a well-ventilated room. Holding the can about ten to twelve inches from the surface, spray across the project in a steady, continuous motion. *Start* or *stop* the spray *off the edge* of the project on the newspaper. This helps to avoid accidental globs, or puddles, of finish on the surface. Continue spraying strips of finish across the project until the surface is covered with a thin, even coat. Avoid overlapping spray strips.

Apply two coats of finish (remember to turn projects that quarter turn between coats just as you did when brushing), rub with finishing pad, and apply two more coats. You will have a thinner finish than if you had brushed or dipped your project, but you can continue more spray coats if you want more depth of finish.

3. It is possible that you have never heard of using a *dipping* technique to apply finish to small woodburned objects. Craftspeople who are familiar with dip glazing in ceramics were our inspiration to try dipping our woodburned bracelets and rings, since we had a large quantity of them to do in a short time. If you would like to try dipping with a similar object, here are the instructions.

Prepare a drying rack (which in our case was a piece of pegboard with metal peg fixtures attached at regular intervals, mounted on the workshop wall). Open the can of finish and mix thoroughly. Use a piece of sturdy wire with a hook bent on one end to dip the bracelet, ring, or what have you down into the finish. That's right—submerge it. (Have a pair of tongs handy to reach into the finish to rescue the project if it should slip off the hook while it is submerged.) Raise the object slowly and hold it over the can a few minutes to allow as much excess finish as possible to drain back into the can. Hang the object on the drying rack over waste paper or a tray, which will catch the drips if there are any. In ten to twelve minutes, use a soft brush to smooth out any bubbles or excess finish that may have accumulated in one spot at the bottom of the object hanging on the rack.

Let the project dry thoroughly (slightly longer than if you had sprayed or brushed). Dip it again and hang it so the "bottom" of the first time is the "top" this time. The steps of rubbing with a finishing pad after every two coats, wiping, and then recoating are the same as though you were spraying or brushing the finish on the project.

Now that you have in mind these three basic steps—I. prepare surface and apply design, II. burn design, III. apply final finish—it is time to read about the various burn strokes and then practice them on a scrap piece of wood. This step is like learning the names of the notes and practicing the scales when you were learning to play the piano.

Once you have this important chapter digested, it will not be necessary to read this information again within the instructions for each project. When you actually get into the woodburning, you should have the basic steps firmly in mind so they will become almost automatic. If there is any variation in a project, the instructions will inform you of that change. Otherwise, take for granted that the three basic steps are always followed with each project.

Familiarize yourself with the *edge, tip, heel, rod,* and *flat plane* of the woodburning pen point as shown in the drawing in chapter 1 on page 4. These names will be used in the burn strokes.

For years, beginners in tole and decorative painting or folk art have been taught the basic brushstrokes that enable them, after practicing, to enjoy method painting. Yet few recognize and tell you that beginning woodburners can follow that example. They can be taught basic burn strokes with the pyrolectric pen that will produce predictable shapes and appearances in woodburned designs. As in the other crafts, practice of these strokes not only encourages better woodburning, but it also increases the ease with which the woodburned design is accomplished. After the basics are mastered, there is plenty of room left for individual experimentation and creation. What are the basic burn strokes?

Dash burn stroke: When the pen point is the proper temperature for the type of surface upon which you are going to burn, set the *whole edge* of the point firmly on the surface where you desire a burned dash. Do not lean the pen's handle to the right or to the left, but hold it in your

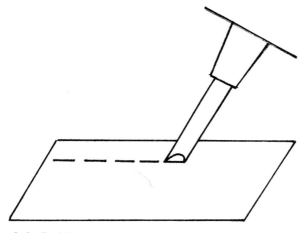

2–2 Dash burn stroke

fingers, as you would a large pencil. Hold the point's edge firmly in that one position until it burns a dash in the wood. This is a matter of seconds.

The longer the edge is held there, the deeper and wider the dash burn will be. The length of the dash will be approximately the length of the pen's point edge. A very thin dash requires just a brief touch of the edge to the surface.

When making a series of uniform-sized, separated dashes, count slowly as you hold the edge on the first burn until it is the desired size and depth. Then, when burning the rest of the dashes, count to the same number each time, and the burned dashes will be relatively uniform, assuming that your point is the same temperature each time and held in the same position.

This is a very easy burn stroke, but it can be used effectively. A line of dashes resembles basting in stitchery. A series of dashes along each side of a narrow, shaded band will give the appearance of saddle stitching. Cross-stitching can be simulated by burning a second dash at an angle over the first, thus making a burned X. Light dashes can also be burned to use for a shading effect or as short animal hair and so on. The examples of this burn stroke are easy to spot when you glance through the project pictures.

Dot burn stroke: Just touching the *tip* of the hot point briefly to the surface will burn a small, light dot. Pressing the tip down more firmly and leaving it in position longer will burn a deeper dot, but this dot is not apt

2–3 Dot burn stroke

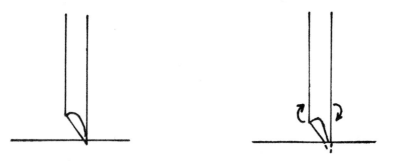

to be an even, circular dot. It will have a triangular shape. If you wish larger dots in a more nearly perfect circular shape, rotate the tip as it burns into the surface. The longer you rotate and burn, the deeper and bigger the dot.

An area filled with spaced dots will appear textured and shaded as you can readily see on Sean's Christmas shoe illustrated on page 26. The closer the burned dots are placed, the darker the shading. Dots are also used to easily burn the outline of letters whose curved lines might make it difficult for the beginner to burn evenly. Mini wild berries, flowers, and balloons are so easy to simulate by burning clusters of dots on appropriate stems.

Line burn stroke: Continuous, even lines are sometimes difficult for the beginner to burn until they have practiced. Yet this burn stroke is used very often in woodburning designs. It helps to keep the surface on which you are burning *movable* so you can turn it with one hand, into the most advantageous position, as you burn the line with the pen held in the other hand. It sounds complicated but it isn't, and you will master this technique quickly with a little practice. (Think about the decoupage beginners who have to learn to turn the decoupage print while the scissors with which they are cutting it are held almost stationary.)

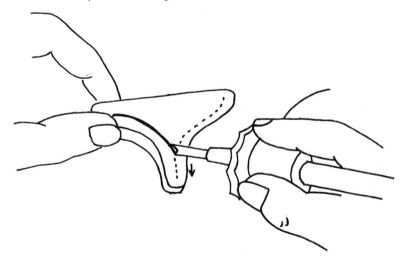

2-4 Line burn stroke

When burning lines, use the whole *edge* of the point, rather than just the tip, as much as possible. This gives more stability and tends to avoid letting the natural resistance of the wood grain change the direction of the line as you burn. Place the whole *edge* of the point on the beginning of your presketched line. Draw the pen point edge firmly and steadily *toward* you along that line. Pushing the pen away from you may seem easier at first, but it makes the grain "fight" the pen and may cause difficulties.

If the line curves, move the object's surface so your pen point edge can follow the curve without having to be repositioned constantly. If the curves are very tight, you may not be able to keep the whole edge in contact with the surface and will have to use only the tip or a portion of the edge in these tight corners. Practice using the whole edge as much as possible.

The faster you draw the point edge along the line, the lighter your burned line will be. At first, you will be well advised to burn each line lightly. It is almost impossible to make a burned line lighter (even with sanding), but it is easy to burn over that line again to make it deeper, darker, and wider as desired. Slanting the point's edge lightly to one side or the other, as you burn, will also widen your burned line. If you want to hesitate or rest, lift the pen from the surface, as a "stopped" pen, held in position on the surface, will burn deeper and make an uneven spot on your line. It takes practice to make fine, even lines that are the mark of the woodburning artist. However, some designs are not negatively influenced by uneven lines. Minor unevenness can be remedied by touching up those areas with the tip of the hot pen or by rubbing them with a finishing pad as explained in the basic woodburning procedures, page 15.

Lines are used extensively in almost all woodburned designs, either as outline or shading with parallel, squared, and grillwork lines. It is possible to use a straight, metal edge ruler to guide the hot pen point edge while you are burning straight lines. This is particularly helpful when burning parallel, squared, or grillwork lines. You will notice sometimes, when you use a metal edge ruler as you burn a line, that the side of the line nearest the ruler may burn very straight, while the other edge of the line may be slightly rough. It is simple to turn the surface around and reburn the line again, using the ruler on the other side so that both edges of the line will be uniformly even.

Petal burn stroke: This is sometimes called the exclamation stroke. To make it, press the *heel* of the hot point on the spot on the surface where you want the widest part of the petal. The longer you hold the heel in position, the deeper and wider the larger portion of the petal will be.

2–5 Petal burn stroke
The x indicates where the stroke is started with the heel of the pen point. Petal burns may be clustered to make simple stars or flowers.

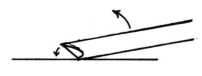

When it is burned to your satisfaction (usually less than a second for small ones), press the pen handle forward until the entire point edge (heel to tip) touches the surface briefly. This will burn a thin tip on the wider base of the petal.

This burn stroke is very useful. Five such burn strokes in a cluster can make up a star or flower, as you see in the drawing. It is the basic stroke for many floral designs and accents that you will discover throughout the book. Plus, it is easy and fast and takes very little practice to master.

Flat plane or broadside shading burn stroke: Hold the pen so the whole *flat plane* on one side of the point is parallel to the surface you want to shade. Press the plane lightly against the surface at the top edge of the area to be shaded and then draw the pen steadily toward you and to the other edge of the "to be shaded" area. The harder you press and the slower you move the pen's plane, the darker the shading will be. Because you are using a relatively large area of the flat plane to burn this shading, the wood grain does not have as much influence upon the direction of your strokes.

Repeat these strokes, placing each burn next to the last. If you overlap the strokes, you will have more variety in the depth of the shade tones. If the edge where you ended your flat plane shading strokes is lighter than the rest, turn the surface around and burn more shading strokes, beginning at the light edge and ending before the middle of the already shaded area, rather than burning clear to the other edge of the area which may already be dark enough.

This stroke usually results in dark shading as you will note on the coasters (2–8, 2–9). Notice one half of the sun's rays and around the fluted edge. The lighter shading on these practice pieces was burned with the mottled shading burn stroke.

Mottled shading burn stroke: In this stroke you are going to use only a quarter of the hot point *edge* and the *tip*. To achieve the most mottling, you must stroke across the grain as much as possible. You can turn the surface you are burning on so it is in the correct position to allow you to accomplish this comfortably.

Think of shading an area on paper with short, back and forth strokes of a soft lead pencil. Starting at one edge of the area to be shaded, lightly stroke the tip and quarter portion of the edge back and forth in short strokes. Do not lift the pen point from the surface as you work. As you stroke across the grain, the tip will burn quickly over the soft areas and be slowed on the harder grain lines, even as you continue guiding the pen back and forth until the entire area is shaded. This momentary hesitation on the grain produces the darker spots that give the mottled effect. Again, the speed with which you move the hot point back and forth over the surface will determine how light or dark this shading is. You can always go back and shade-burn certain areas again if they are not dark enough for your purposes.

You will find this mottled shading very useful because it affords you varying shades of brown in your designs, it adds texture interest, and is very fast and easy to do. It can be used on very large or small areas. Shade in the same manner, except go with the grain, if you want a less mottled shading.

Rod burn stroke: The rod of the pyrolectric pen, between the point and the protective cork, becomes hot when the pen is in use. If this rod is held across the sharp edge of a wood surface, it will burn a half circle groove into the wood. The longer it is held in one place, the deeper the burn.

You can also burn longer grooves in from the edge of plaques to simulate wear and distressing.

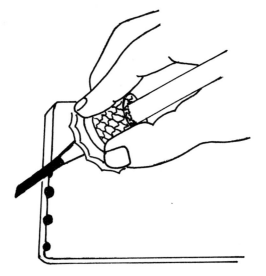

2–6 Rod burn stroke

V-edge burn stroke: If you wish V-shaped, small grooves along the edge of the wood, hold the sharp *edge* of the point across the edge of the wood. Hold it in position until it burns a V-shaped groove into the wood.

Maybe you are not as "Scotch" as I am, but I have always hated to practice on scrap wood that will be thrown away. Sometimes the practice pieces turn out to be very nice and worth saving. Yet I know, as you do, that practice of woodburning strokes is necessary for anyone before tackling a large involved project. The mini basswood plaques (7/16" thick) from O. P. Crafts were my answer. They are inexpensive, and you can finish them as coasters when you are through practicing burning them. Besides the mini-cornered ones that are pictured here, there are mini-rounds (3½" diameter) and mini-elliptics (5⅜" x 3⅜") that could also be burned with this practice pattern and later used as coasters. You will need to burn the design, apply water-resistant wood finish, and add

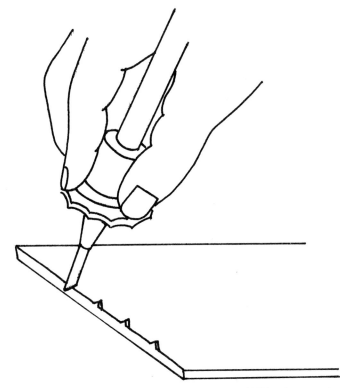

2-7 V-Edge burn stroke

2-8 This piece of woodburning illustrates why practice is needed. Note the inaccuracy of the border measurement and the unevenness of the burned lines that could have been remedied. Remeasuring the border line and sketching it with more accuracy, then making that line into a wider burned band to conceal the original defective line would have improved the appearance of the workmanship.

2-9 This second practice piece shows the unevenness of the lines is already improving. But measurement and burning exactly on the sketched lines are still not as accurate as desired. If those visible pencil lines are not erased before the finish is applied, they will always continue to show, as you can see here.

a thin layer of cork or felt to their back side to protect the tabletop if you wish to use them as coasters.

This particular basic pattern involves practicing the short lines, dots, petal, shading, V-edge, and rod burn strokes. The lined areas indicate shading and the dotted lines boundary areas that should be dotted completely. Don't be shy. Add more burned details on this basic pattern if you feel more is needed to make the design pleasing to you.

This small ash basket is another example, as its woodburned trim was the result of a practice session. Certainly, with my limited drawing ability, even though I had practiced the burn strokes, when I wanted to burn more or less freehand and not trace a pattern, I hesitated to work on a costly wooden piece at first. This unfinished kindling basket stood by the fireplace and caught my eye.

After burning a few simple designs (which strictly used the simplest burn strokes as you can determine from the drawing), shading here and there, and applying finish, the basket looked so attractive that it gradu-

2-10 A basic outline pattern for practicing burn strokes.

2-11 Practice makes perfect and it also decorates an unfinished ash basket of humble origin.

ated to serving as a plant holder on the kitchen table. The finished basket (with a liner) is even occasionally used as a pot luck supper basket and draws a lot of attention and comments. Someday you might like to make a summer basket purse with a woodburned design on it. A lot of different shaped baskets are unfinished when sold in the stores and are made of ash, which makes a good practice material for the woodburner to work on anytime.

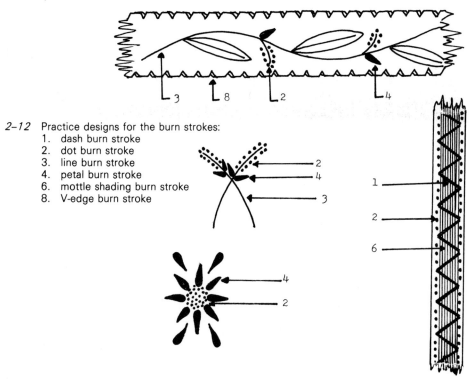

2-12 Practice designs for the burn strokes:
1. dash burn stroke
2. dot burn stroke
3. line burn stroke
4. petal burn stroke
6. mottle shading burn stroke
8. V-edge burn stroke

Just for review, look at Sean's Christmas shoe and identify the burn strokes that were used on it. Notice how the dots fill in the areas around the letters and toe design to outline them more easily than could have been done with curved, woodburned lines. It is a beginner's project, though it may not look like it.

2-13   Sean's wooden shoe, that serves as a Christmas stocking, illustrates the use of basic burn strokes.

2-14   Stalking Tiger by Regina Petrutis
Designs may be burned on very thin sheets of balsam wood or mahogany. Mounting them on heavier wooden plaques will give them more stability. Note the difference created between the vertical line shading on the top of the background in this picture and the horizontal mottled shade burning on the "ground."
Picture courtesy Regina Petrutis

3 "EASY DOES IT" CRAFT PROJECTS

How about the use of traced patterns in woodburning? Very few of the projects in this book are entirely made by the typical "toy" woodburning method, which would be 1) trace design on wood and 2) burn the outline. Once you develop woodburning into a craft, you will want to add your personal touches of more shading or accents—even when a basic traced pattern is used. Several basic outline patterns are included in chapter 4 and there are tracing projects in this chapter.

Let's make use of your creativity right from the beginning, even as you develop your skill at burning the various strokes. Try this exercise with a butterfly pattern. Trace the basic butterfly outline onto different pieces of wood. In the pictured ones, we used 5" x 5" weathered alderwood plaques. (Have you noticed that I included a different pattern than the one used on my small plaques pictured, so you would not be tempted to copy mine exactly? Just another try to encourage you to develop your own style.)

Woodburn one butterfly's outline entirely with just line burns of different widths, as you probably would have woodburned it as a child might. Now, after outline burning the second butterfly, shade certain areas of that butterfly with evenly spaced dashes and dots as indicated on the pattern. Next, burn the third butterfly, using mottled shading, dashes, dots, petal, line burn strokes—wherever you decide they would look pleasing. Compare the three. If you added your own creative touches to the third butterfly, nine chances out of ten, you will like it best!

My practice butterfly plaques eventually became paperweights with

3–1 Weathered alderwood plaques, approximately 5" X 5", were used for these examples of a beginner's practice exercise. The top right plaque was entirely burned by lines of varying widths. The top left plaque features shading by lines in grillwork with burned squares, dots, petals, and dashes added to the basic outline. The other two show the use of different acrylic wood stains and colors, brushed into certain areas of the basic burned outline to add color.

3–2 Sketch your own or use this butterfly pattern to practice.

the addition of a layer of dark felt on their back sides. They function beautifully, having just enough weight to hold the stacks of loose paper in place on my desk.

This exercise should give you practice, confidence in your own ability, and will explain why, in some of the photographs, the finished projects will have touches that were not detailed on the pattern. Always feel free to add or subtract any details from the patterns that you like. You are the woodburner!

Black Duck Oval Plaque

This 6" x 9" oval redwood plaque (with a precarved and stained edge) begged for an outdoor theme design. Since the figure of the wood was

3–3 Black Duck on oval plaque was designed by Lisa Petranoff and woodburned by Elaine Broadwater.

3–4 Tracing pattern of Black Duck by Lisa Petranoff.

not obvious, would not detract from a design with finer detail nor deflect the pen point, the intricacies of the duck's feathers are no problem, even to the beginning woodburner.

If you use this pattern, designed by Lisa Petranoff, follow the steps outlined in the general procedures in chapter 2. Note that on this duck plaque, the use of semigloss finish avoided the high shine that might reflect too much light and detract from the texture of the woodburned duck's feathers. You might like to make a companion plaque for the Black Duck using the Osprey pattern in chapter 4, which was also designed by Lisa.

D.B., The Puppy

During the time that we were woodburning projects for this book, someone gave George a new puppy. She was promptly christened D.B. (initials for Daddy's Baby) for obvious reasons, but she soon had all of us enchanted. My secretary, Lisa, could not resist drawing D.B., which

3–5 D. B., The Puppy. Designed by Lisa Petranoff and wood-burned by Elaine Broadwater.

naturally led to my trying to translate that drawing [see 3–6] onto a wood plaque with the woodburning pen.

For anyone who has practiced woodburning long enough to accomplish tiny, thin freehand strokes of the hot pen, these could be used to shade and simulate the dog's hair, and this project would be easy. However, for the beginner to trace each and every hair line onto the wood would not only be difficult but tedious and frustrating as well. So why not try this simpler method if you would like to woodburn this puppy on a plaque.

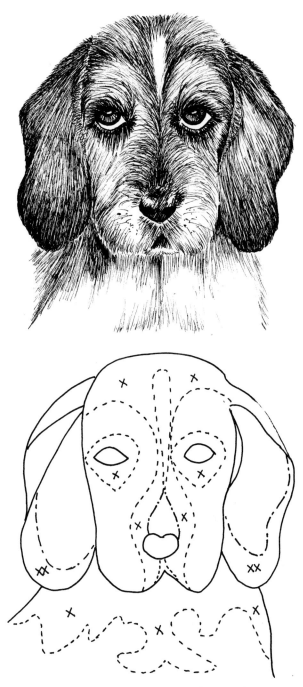

3-6 Pen and ink sketch of D.B. by Lisa Petranoff.

3-7 Use a basic outline pattern for simplified burning.

1) Select a plaque to use, similar to the alderwood one pictured, whose distinctive figure already suggests line and shading. 2) Trace the pattern 3–7 onto your plaque. *Line* burn the main outline indicated by solid lines. Then use short line strokes to shade the X areas within the dotted lines. XX means darker shading. 3) Consult drawing 3–6 and add more light, burned strokes to your plaque freehand. Follow the direction and density of the ink pen strokes in the drawing. How many do you burn? As many as you like to satisfy your own ideas of what looks best.

Alderwood darkens slightly when wood finish is applied, and the similarity of the brown tones of the woodburning and the wood on my plaque suggested the use of a dark band around the plaque. This band appeared to contain or restrict the burned sketch of the puppy and increased its importance. Your plaque might not need this touch, but if it does you can paint or woodburn the outside edge.

Remember to rub your woodburned areas with a fine sanding pad before you paint the edge or apply the wood finish. We used semigloss, clear wood finish on this plaque too, since it was our intention to make the puppy's coat gleam, not shine.

In the pattern section in chapter 4, you will find an outline pattern of a rabbit that can be traced and then freehand burn strokes are used to give it some fluffy hair in the right spots.

Pharaoh and His Pet

3–8   Pharaoh. Designed by Lisa Petranoff and woodburned by Elaine Broadwater.

The exhibits of King Tut's treasures started quite a rage for Egyptian artwork. By keeping the designs relatively simple and stylized, we felt we could include some Egyptian-influenced patterns for beginners here. When Lisa drew the patterns, she used lines for all the shading as a pen and ink artist is apt to do. However, if you have not mastered fine, even lines with the woodburning pen as yet, you will find it easier to *line burn* just the main lines. Then use *mottle shade burning* for the areas in the

3–9 Pharaoh's Pet. Designed by Lisa Petranoff and woodburned by Elaine Broadwater.

3–10 Tracing pattern for Pharaoh by Lisa Petranoff.

3–11 Tracing pattern for Pharaoh's Pet by Lisa Petranoff.

drawing where she used line shading. This same mottled shading, in different tones, is used to fill in the background and make the image appear sharper.

These two patterns were woodburned on two entirely different type plaques to show that you need not limit yourself to any one use of these patterns. The Pharaoh is pictured on a classic California redwood plaque, 11/16" thick, that was prebordered to accent the woodburning within it. The Pharaoh's Pet is on a 5" x 7" alderwood plaque with tooled edges. Notice the difference between the colors of the two woods, although they were finished alike. You will also notice that the darker half of the redwood (a natural part of its figure) was used to appear as a shadow on that side of the Pharaoh. The procedure is just as described in the general instructions.

A pattern for a female counterpart of the Pharaoh is included in chapter 4. Be forewarned and practice your woodburning before you attempt the woodburning of that lady. It is more difficult than Pharaoh or his pet.

Florawood Planters

3-12 Woodburned Florawood planter, model II.

Years ago when I saw these Florawood planters, which are made of basswood with a fitted plastic liner, at a craft show, I fell in love with them. Since then I have seen the different Florawood models painted, carved, decoupaged, and gold-leafed—but not woodburned. So that became my challenge. Model II and IV each have a slight curve to their sides, but still turned out to be an easy woodburning feat. Do not try to trace the pattern on the curved surface. Rather use your pencil, ruler, and compass to measure the pattern and transfer it to the wood planter with light pencil marks.

Florawood II has eight panels so each of the two pattern designs is used on four alternate panels. These panels of basswood have very little

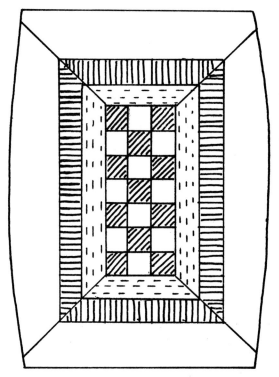
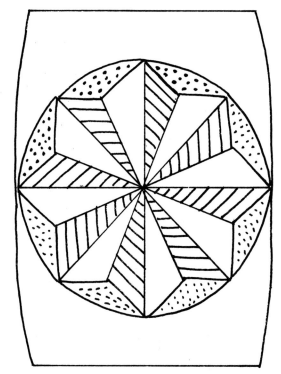

3–13   Pattern guide for panels of Florawood planter II.

3–14   Woodburned Florawood planter, model II.

3–14A   Woodburned Florawood Planter, model IV.

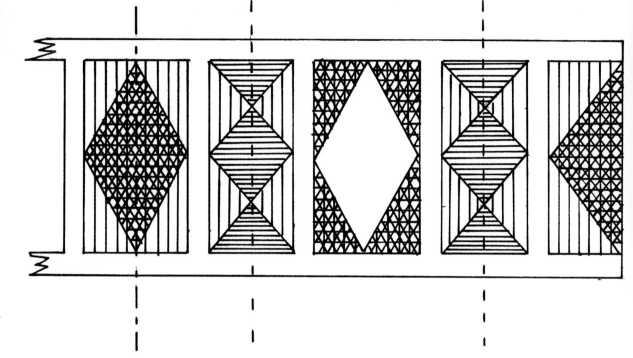

3–15 Pattern guide for wraparound band on Florawood planter IV.

figure and are very light colored, so after the woodburning of the panel designs was completed the entire planter was *mottle shaded* lightly with the woodburning pen. Maybe you will decide to leave yours unshaded and lighter colored as we did Florawood IV.

The design on Florawood IV is a continuous wraparound band. (Only half is shown in drawing 3–15.) The dotted lines through the band in the pattern indicate the ridge joints on the planter and are intended to help you space the design. Beside the design band and a small design on the backboard of the planter, the rest of the area was left unburned and finished with wood finish as usual.

A Quote with Owls

In the midst of a busy, harrowing day, a glance at this, one of my favorite sayings (mounted on my office wall), provides momentary comic relief. Thought we could use a light moment here too—right about now. It is true that the owl motif is currently featured in many craft projects and books, magazines and newspaper advertising, and almost everywhere you look. It is relatively easy to find one to use as a tracing pattern for woodburning, if that is your desire. However, rather than copy someone else's lovely owls, I decided to use my own version of this comical family of Father, Mother, Little Brother, and Sister Owl to accompany the calligraphic quote that I found in a craft supply shop. Just call them my attempt at a little nonsense.

36

3-16 An encouragement to humor, Quote with Owl Family.

When making this plaque, the procedure varies from the usual basic three steps only in that the quote is glued in position after the woodburning and painting are completed—before the wood finish is applied. Extra coats of finish are needed to completely submerge the quote, as you would in a decoupage technique.

If you lack sketching talent, a humorous interpretation of popular motifs is a good place to begin developing your ability. If it looks funny, people think you intended that effect!

Tired of tracing? Draw your design directly on the wood. It will not be long after you start woodburning that you will try to eliminate as much tracing as possible. You will start measuring and drawing your burning design directly onto the unfinished wood surface. Use light pencil strokes and keep that large eraser handy to rub out your mistakes and excess pencil lines.

At this point do not let your lack of drawing ability inhibit you. You can design effective woodburning projects with just geometric figures that

3-17 Tracing pattern for owl family if you cannot sketch your own.

are easily drawn with the aid of a ruler and compass, even though you may not be able to draw landscapes, portraits, and so on to your own satisfaction.

When the printed pattern in this book is in actual size, you can use your ruler and compass to measure the lines on the drawing and transfer them to the wood surface. Or trace the main outline and fill in the other details freehand.

Personalized Coat Hanger

3-18 A personalized coat hanger features the use of basic burn strokes in geometric designs.

Unfinished wooden coat hangers, like the one pictured, are available in some craft supply shops. This is an example of a project that makes use of simple lines and circles to comprise a finished design that personalizes the coat hanger. Maybe you would prefer to put MR or MS in the center rather than the actual initials. Notice drawing 3–20 and you will see how any two initials can be drawn to fit into the center circle.

On the pictured hanger, acrylic paint was applied in some areas to add color and further accent to this design. It would have been just as effective with only the woodburned tones of brown, but I had used the hanger for some time in its unfinished state and it was water stained. The acrylic paint concealed these defects that could not be sanded away.

To some, this hanger may have a masculine look. Perhaps you would rather woodburn a floral motif in the center and use script letters spelling out a full name on either side of the center.

The Burned Baker's Dozen

Christmas ornaments and decorations are always perennial favorites for craft projects. If you are a troop leader, Sunday School teacher, bazaar worker, recreational director, or just an avid crafter, you are

3-20 Adapt blocky initials for the center circle.

3-19 One-half hanger pattern guide, to be reversed for other half of hanger.

39

probably always looking for something different. How would you like a dozen or more ideas for Christmas, using supplies you can purchase at your local craft supply shop or that can be adapted to wood pieces you may already have? Of course, since the subject of this book is woodburning, these projects will feature just that! And the best part is that you can creatively use these ideas for your group activities with any age person of either sex. Naturally, you will not attempt to do woodburning with children who have not reached the age of reason. Plus, the artistically inclined in the group can improvise and add their own touches while the others will accomplish very satisfactory projects by just following these directions.

Listed here are the materials and tools that you will use regardless of which ornament you choose to make. A few additional items may be needed for some of the projects, and these will be listed in the directions for that specific ornament. (If you are unfamiliar with any of the supplies, see Supply Sources in the back of this book.)

Materials: woodburning pen, acrylic paints, sanding and finishing pads, wood finish, alderwood rings, crescents and spandrels (see individual directions for size and #), eye screws (½" long and as thin as possible), pencil, ruler, liner paintbrush, white craft glue, and finish applicator.

General instructions:

1. "Rub down" unfinished alderwood pieces (spandrels, crescents, or rings) with the medium sanding pad or #400 sandpaper to smooth them slightly if necessary. A thorough sanding on the edges of the spandrels is not required because those edges will be burned. Lightly pencil sketch the desired design or guiding marks on the wood. Tracing a pattern in this case is not desirable because the sizes of the wooden pieces may vary slightly from the pattern, and it is a bit difficult to trace around the curves of the rings. In any case, the lines are so simple that they can be drawn directly on the wood with ease by following the directions and consulting the accompanying drawings for each.

2. If you are using the pyrolectric pen that requires a light bulb in the plug series tap, use a 100-watt bulb to woodburn on unfinished alderwood. If you are burning on a softer wood, you may want to switch to a 75-watt bulb. Dash, dot, petal, line, and rod burn strokes are all that are used so the projects are suitable for the beginning woodburners. *Closely supervise children while they are woodburning.*

3. When the design lines are all burned, remember to rub the entire piece with a fine sanding pad or very fine steel wool. This will smooth the surface to the extent needed for ease in applying finish. Wipe the woodburned piece with a soft cloth or paper towel to remove the sanding dust and loose carbon particles.

If additional color, besides the woodburned brown, is desired, thin your acrylic paints with just enough water to use them as a stain for a transparent effect. This provides desired color on the wood, but will also allow the grain to show through. Try to avoid filling the design lines with paint anyhow, as it dulls the rich brown of the woodburning. Screw the eyelet screw into the top of the piece to provide a handy handle when you are applying wood finish to the ornament.

4. Be sure the paint is thoroughly dry before applying two coats of semigloss or gloss wood finish—with appropriate drying time between coats. The finish may be applied with a sponge applicator, a brush, or by dipping. If you have a large number of ornaments to finish at one time, the quickest way is to dip them. Hold them by a wire hook (make one out of a paper clip) through the eyelet screw in their top.

When the second coat of finish is thoroughly dry, rub the entire piece lightly with a fine sanding pad. Apply one thin coat of finish for the final gloss.

Spandrel Christmas Tree

3–21 Spandrel Christmas tree ornaments.

(Needs a #7-092-1-76 spandrel.)

1. Read these directions, consult the drawings, and then pencil sketch lines on the wooden spandrel that you feel you will need for guidance in woodburning. You may want to start on the bottom of the spandrel. This gives a beginner practice *line* burning, while making the grillwork design there. Please look at drawing 3–22. These steps correspond to the letters on that drawing. a. Burn horizontal lines ⅛" apart. b. Burn vertical lines ⅛" apart. c. Burn diagonal lines from left to right ⅛" apart. d. Burn diagonal lines from right to left until entire bottom is covered by grillwork design.

2. (Please see drawing 3–22 where each of the following steps is identified.) *Line* burn the outline of a stylized tree ⅛" from edge of spandrel on the front flat surface.

3. Burn the star at the top of the tree with *petal* burn stroke. (Look

3–20A Fifteen Christmas ornaments, all woodburned.

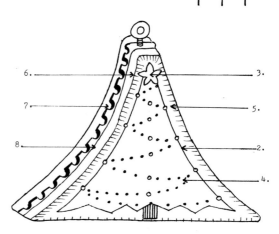

3–22 Woodburning steps for spandrel Christmas tree, including the grillwork on the bottom of the spandrel. Note that the numbers and letters correspond to steps in the directions.

at drawing 2–5 again in chapter 2 in the basic burn stroke information.)

4. Vary between light and medium size *dot* burns for garland and simulated ornaments on the tree.

5. Burn light, short *dashes* on the surface, along the edges, to border the tree.

6. Lightly pass the hot rod of the pen around the sharp edges of the spandrel to create a fine burned edge all around it.

7. Hold the rod straight across the ridge that runs up the spandrel

sides. *Rod* burn evenly spaced, half-rounded grooves along both sides on that ridge.

8. Burn a fine line on both sides of the grooved ridge on both sides of the spandrel.

9. Add color with thinned acrylic paint if desired. The two finished examples of this ornament show the different effects achieved by either painting only the tree or only the background.

Attach eyelet screw and apply finish as directed in the general instructions. After a little practice, it will take you approximately 15 minutes to woodburn an ornament. And we can abbreviate the directions a little more from here on because you have the basic idea firmly in mind.

Spandrel Christmas Bell

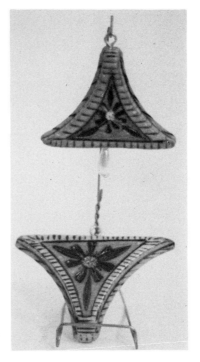

3-23 Spandrel Christmas bell ornament (top). Reversed, without bell clapper, it becomes a pointed floral ornament.

(Needs any size spandrel and corresponding size teardrop pearl.)

1. Pencil sketch the guidance lines ¼" apart on the bottom of the spandrel according to drawing 3–24. *Line* burn "chevron" design on bottom of spandrel and up the sides.

3-24 Chevron design for bottom of bell spandrel.

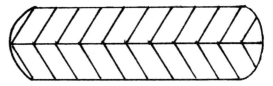

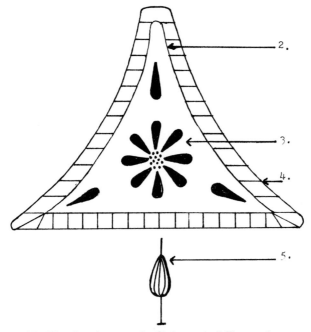

3–25 Woodburning steps for Christmas bell. The numbers correspond to steps in the directions.

2. Please see drawing 3–25. *Line* burn triangle on flat front of spandrel, ⅛" from its edges.

3. Burn flower in center of that triangle with *dot* and *petal* burn strokes. Burn leaves in each of the three corners of the triangle with *petal* stroke.

4. Burn *dashes* on area between triangle and spandrel edges at even intervals.

5. Paint and finish the bell before inserting long pin through the teardrop pearl and on into the middle of the spandrel bottom to simulate a bell clapper.

As you can see in the picture, you can omit the clapper, reverse the spandrel, and have a pointed floral ornament.

Scenic or Symbolic Spandrels

These can be made on any size spandrel or similar piece of wood. They give you a chance to burn almost completely freehand. Pencil sketch a simple design on the wood and use the beginner's burn strokes to decorate. (See drawing 3–26 for possible design ideas.) You will readily recognize in this drawing the burn strokes used. *Dots* were burned on the toe of the stocking to form the words "Joy" and "Hi" and on the star outline. Light *line* strokes burned the pine trees and sun rays, while heavier *lines* were used for the bricks and blocks and others. When you are finished burning, paint and finish as directed in the general instructions.

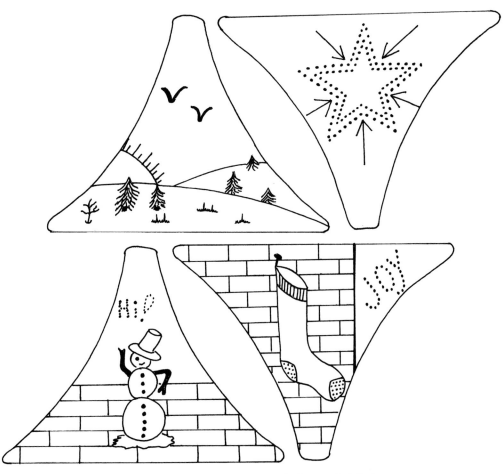

3-26 Design ideas for simple scenic or symbolic spandrel Christmas ornaments.

Double Spandrel Eye of God

(Needs two spandrels of matching size.)

1. You may woodburn the two pieces separately and then glue them together *if* you keep the lines evenly measured so they match. Or you can glue the two spandrels together, as in drawing 3–28, and wait until the glue is dry before woodburning. That is the easier way.

2. Glance at the drawing from time to time for guidance in the following steps. *Line* burn ⅛" from edge, around the outside of the flat, front surface. Then burn another line inside that first one, ¼" from the edge. Burn dots between the first and second lines.

3. *Line* burn a four-pointed star. Then *dash* burn the area around it within the lines. Shade the star with the pen tip if desired.

4. *Rod* burn the ridge on all sides of the spandrel. Use the hot rod to lightly burn all the sharp edges of the spandrel.

5. Now choose the areas where you would like to paint in colors and do it. Or you can just rely on the natural browns of the wood and the burned lines to provide enough interest. After you have fastened the eyelet screw in the top, do not forget to put on the wood finish.

3–27 Double spandrel Eye of God Christmas ornament.

3–28 Woodburning guide for Eye of God ornament.

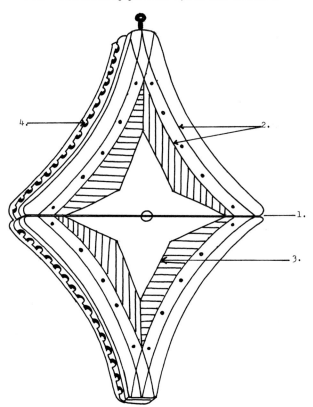

Double Spandrel Lantern

(Needs two spandrels of matching size.)

1. Glue spandrels together and let the glue dry thoroughly. As you can see in drawing 3–30, the steps for this ornament are similar to the ones for the Eye of God. Any differences are noted in the following steps.

2. *Line* burn as in step 2 for Eye of God, except there are no dots to be burned in the resulting band.

3. The design is varied by *line* burning grillwork in the band around the outside edge.

4. *Rod* burn evenly spaced grooves on the ridge running over the top spandrel only.

5. Use burned dots to decorate "lampshade" with a star and in the area around a burned candle flame. Now proceed with the finishing procedure as usual.

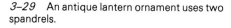

3–29   An antique lantern ornament uses two spandrels.

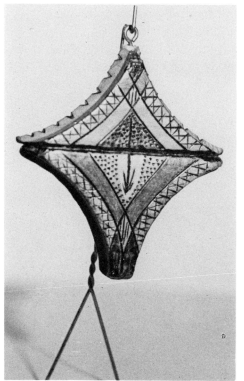

3–30   Woodburning guide for lantern ornament.

Quartered Double Spandrel

3–31 Quartered design is burned on two spandrels of equal size to make this ornament.

(Needs two spandrels of matching size.)

1. Glue the spandrels together as shown in drawing 3–32. The edges may be trimmed with a hobby knife to an exact fit if necessary.

2. Pencil sketch lines to quarter the entire piece and *line* burn those lines.

3. Use *dot* burn to outline star. Fill in that quarter's background with dots, clustered closer together near and around the star and farther apart toward the edges.

4. Use *dot, petal,* and *line* burn strokes to burn flowers in two side quarter sections. For variation, try burning holly leaves, poinsettia, and so on in these quarters.

5. *Shade* burn the sides of the spandrels.

6. In this quarter section, *line* burn evenly spaced lines to make a grillwork design. Remember, that is the way the bottom of the spandrel Christmas tree was burned.

Why not just apply wood finish on this one and skip adding extra color with acrylics? You can vary this design by using different simple symbols in the quarter sections and adding *dot* burned script.

3–32 Woodburning guide for quartered spandrel ornament.

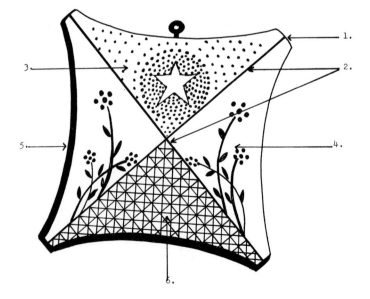

Wooden Basket of Quilled Flowers

3-33 A wooden basket of quilled flowers would be appropriate for an Easter or Christmas ornament.

(Needs spandrel of any size and matching size crescent.)

Crescents are actually different sized partial pieces cut from an alder-wood ring. In this project you will want one that is more than half a circle so that it will resemble the handle of a basket. It also must fit properly onto the top of the spandrel basket. You may need to trim the bottom with a sharp knife to make it fit. If you do not have the proper size crescent, cut one from a complete ring. (Save the little piece from the ring that will be left over. You can sand it smooth, woodburn a design on it, and then attach a pinback to make it an unusual jewelry pin.) It is easier to wait until you have both crescent and spandrel woodburned before you glue them together. See drawing 3-34.

3-34 Woodburning guide for basket.

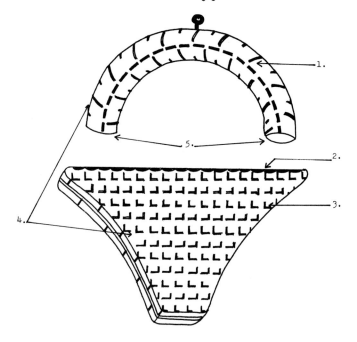

1. *Dash* burn around and across the crescent "handle." If you hold the crescent firmly with a pliers or a large tweezers, you can turn it easily while you work and will avoid bringing your fingers into contact with the hot point.

2. *Rod* burn evenly spaced grooves around the top edge of the spandrel to simulate the fluted edge of the basket. *Shade* burn the flat, top surface between the grooves.

3. *Dash* burn horizontal rows of evenly spaced dashes ⅛" apart. Then *dash* burn at alternate positions vertically between the horizontal rows to simulate weaving.

4. Lightly *shade* burn over the entire basket (crescent and spandrel).

5. Glue the crescent handle to top of woodburned spandrel. Also glue several quilled flowers in position on the basket as in the picture. If you are not a quiller, you can substitute tiny velvet forget-me-nots, dried star flowers, beaded miniature poinsettia, or other ready-made blossoms that are available in your local craft supply shop.

6. Attach an eyelet screw on top of the handle. We did not put wood finish on this basket so it would retain its rustic look, but if you prefer it smooth and shiny, you can apply finish as usual.

Pine Bough Wreath

3-35 Pine bough wreath ornament.

(Needs any size small ring, miniature figurine, and narrow ribbon.) See drawing 3-36.

1. *Line* burn two semicircle "branches" on the face of the ring.

2. *Dash* burn smaller stems from those branches, evenly spaced.

3. *Dash* burn needles of graduated sizes on each small stem.

4. Finish as in the general directions. This project is particularly suited

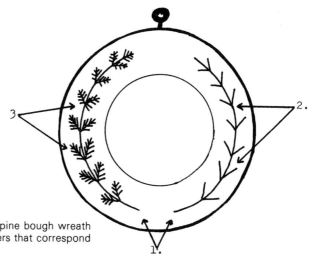

3-36 Woodburning guide for pine bough wreath on alderwood ring shows numbers that correspond to steps in the directions.

to the dipping method of applying finish. Attach a ribbon bow on the ornament after the finish is dry.

This design can be adapted to any size ring and varied by finishing it natural or applying green acrylic stain over just the needle area. Or change the type of miniatures used within the ring.

Wood Beauty with Poinsettia Accent

(Needs a 3¼" or smaller ring.) See drawing 3-37.

3-37 A woodburned poinsettia adds to the natural beauty of the alderwood ring.

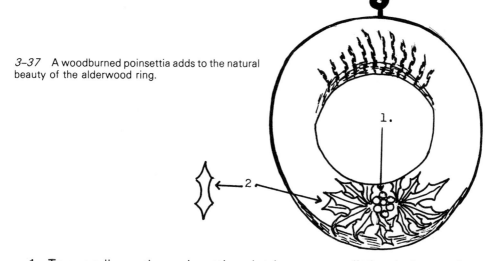

1. To woodburn the poinsettia, *dot* burn seven little circles at the bottom of the ring for the center of the flower.

2. Make a paper pattern of an elongated holly leaf. Trace around it on the ring, placing it in different positions and in as many positions as necessary to create a circular flower around the burned dotted center. *Line* burn this flower's petals. Attach eyelet screw to top of ring.

51

3. Stain most of the petals a red color, then a few outside petals green to simulate leaves. Touch the center with yellow acrylic paint between the dots.

4. Proceed with the finishing, as the finish will enhance the natural wood grain showing on the ring.

Variations: a. Mount a miniature figure in the ring or add a narrow ribbon bow at the bottom. b. Rather than just making one poinsettia at the base of the ring, use the same paper pattern of the holly leaf to draw poinsettia all around the ring as a wreath. Position the pattern and trace it at different angles on the ring so the whole ring is covered. You can make this "foliage" as thick as you desire, or you can space them so more background of the wood will show. (See the "sparsely foliaged" ring pictured in photograph 3–38.)

3–38   Add a miniature and bow for variety.

3–39   Space the poinsettia leaves to allow wood grain to show on a Christmas ornament.

When you *line* burn all the leaves, put vein markings in the center of each. *Dot* burn berries at regular intervals in clusters between the leaves. If you want color, stain the leaves green and circle the berries with a thin line of red. Attach eyelet screw in the top and finish as usual. If you make this wreath of a #7-013-2-76 Woodring Craft ring, omit the eyelet screw and make a large Christmas napkin ring or a small child's bracelet.

Wood Overlay Holy Scene

3-40 Woodburned Holy Scene with veneer paper overlay.

(Needs #7-0 1 3-2-00 ring and three colors of Veneer Touch® wood inlay paper.) When you are woodburning this design on the ring, see drawing 3–41.

1. Lightly pencil sketch the outline of the stable on the ring. Where the roof appears to hang out from the ring on the drawing, it is an indication that you are to draw it around the side of the ring.

3–41 Woodburning guide for stable of Holy Scene.

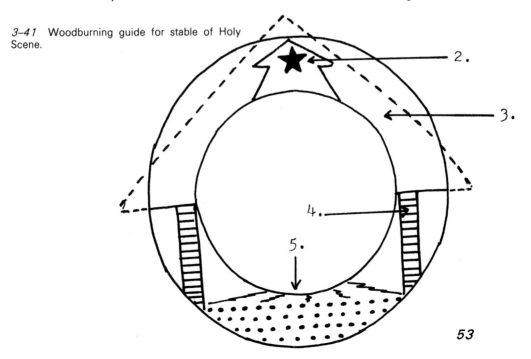

2. Use five *petal* burn strokes in a cluster to form the star at the top of the stable roof.

3. *Dash* or short *line* burn diagonal strokes to simulate the straw on the roof. Remember to continue the strokes around the curve of the ring in the area of the roof.

4. *Line* burn the poles that appear to hold up the roof and *shade* burn or make *dashes* between the 3/16" wide lines that make up the poles.

5. *Dot* and *shade* burn at the bottom of the ring to simulate stones and earth.

6. Attach eyelet screw in top of ring and finish the ring before gluing the overlay paper scene within the circle. You will have time to make the encircled scene while the wood finish is drying on the ring.

1. See drawing 3–42. Trace the outside outline of the background pattern on the back of a piece of white birch wood inlay paper. Cut out

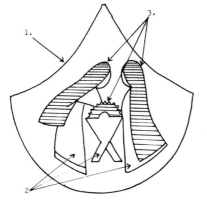

3–42 Veneer paper overlay pattern for center of ornament.

two pieces of this pattern and glue them together with the right sides out.

2. Trace complete outline of the three figures on the back of some walnut wood inlay paper. Cut them out and glue them in position on the white birch background.

3. Trace the portions of the figures that are lined on the pattern onto the back of mahogany wood inlay paper. Cut them out and glue them in position on the walnut paper figures. This is an overlay design so there is no need to try to make them look inlaid as you would when using real wood veneer.

Apply glue to the bottom edge of the overlay inset design and glue it in position inside the finished woodburned ring.

Woodburned Arte Frame with Tie Tack Collection

These alderwood arte frames are great when it comes to displaying a small collection of miniature items such as my antique silver tie tacks. There are many ways you can woodburn the frame to add interest and importance to the miniatures enclosed. The thing I liked about the de-

3-43 Woodburned arte frame enclosing a tie tack collection.

sign in the drawing was that it could be accomplished in a short time and required no tracing. If you would rather trace, another arte frame pattern is in chapter 4.

1. Normally, the openings in these arte frames require a little more sanding than the surface. Here you particularly want the wood smooth so it will look attractive when finished and contrast with the texture of the woodburning. So take a little extra care in sanding.

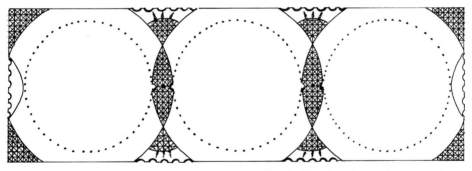

3-44 Woodburning guide for arte frame.

2. Use a compass and pencil to draw a circle around the openings that is ½" larger than they are. Just as you see in the drawing, those circles will "run" off the frame's edge in places. Where the circles intersect between the openings will be what I call an "hourglass" shape.

Draw the short curved line in the places indicated on the drawing (at top and bottom, at each side of hourglass). Measure and pencil dot ⅛" reference points for the grillwork.

3. You are ready to burn. *Rod* burn small, evenly spaced grooves on the edges of the arte frame in the areas indicated on the drawing. Then *line* burn your circles and curved lines.

Use a metal edge ruler to guide the hot edge of the point as you burn the grillwork in the areas indicated on the drawing. In this project you are using an ⅛" measurement, so you will first burn ⅛" squares and then diagonal lines across them for the grillwork. Such a small grillwork gives a very dark brown appearance and contrasts sharply with the natural wood tones around the opening that you have left. *Mottle shade* burn the area between the short curved lines and the rod-burned grooves on the edge of the hourglass shapes and at each end. Do not forget the three little *petal* burns that accent the ends of the hourglass shapes.

4. Proceed with finishing the wood as in the general instructions in chapter 2—rub down, apply wood finish (two coats), rub down, more wood finish.

5. Cut out three circles of corregated cardboard that will fit snugly within the openings. Glue a covering circle on them of a slightly textured fabric that will contrast with the smooth wooden ring around the opening. Glue the covered circles in position in the arte frame and mount your miniatures within the openings.

You can mount coins in these openings by using two cardboard circles in each opening. On the top circle, cut out a center opening slightly smaller than the coin to be mounted. When you push the coin down into that opening, it will stay in place. A drop of craft glue behind the coin provides even more security and can be peeled off it you ever want to use the coin for another purpose.

3-45 Another arte frame that is entwined with a woodburned grapevine. The pattern is included in chapter 4.

Add Woodburning Accents to Other Craft Projects

Just you wait—you will do it too after you have been woodburning a while. When you are participating in other craft activities, you will keep discovering new ways in which touches of woodburning will add something extra.

This little recessed frame from Clauss Manufacturing is ideal to frame papier tole designs. However, in the case of the print that we had used,

3–46 A woodburned frame enhances a papier tole scene.

the frame seemed too formal around the completed papier tole of the aged wooden trough and pump. *Mottled shading,* burned around the inside walls of the recess, looked almost like the wood in the trough. A hot, *flat plane* pressed along the ridges on the front of the unfinished frame softened and added a rougher texture to them. A ½"-wide band of *mottle shaded* triangles around the outside might not have been necessary. But they drew the eye upward to the picture and avoided using too much solid shading, which might have made the small frame appear too heavy.

The final touch was to paint leaf green between the rich, burned brown bands to really give the feeling of springtime to the entire frame.

Since you can use the pyrolectric pen on paper too, the edges of the print can be shaded.

Woodburned Flower on a Candlestick

One of the real joys of learning to use woodburned designs as part of the finishing technique on craft projects is finding out what a wide variety of objects lend themselves effectively to this method. This unfinished wooden candlestick (O. P. Crafts #3545, 3⅛" diameter x 2¾" high) standing on the shelf in a craft supply shop just naturally attracted my eye with its nostalgic look. But I made a mistake by only buying one at that time. Later, when it was finished, it occurred to me how much simpler it would be to finish two candlesticks at the same time.

Some beginner woodburners shy away from curved surfaces or three-dimensional shaped objects because they foresee difficulties in tracing

3-47 Combine woodburning with decorative painting.

a pattern onto this type of surface. There is a solution. Measure and draw a simple design right on the wood. The ability to draw a pencil line, either straight or curved, is all you need in this project.

1. See drawing 3–48. Remove the candle cup from the base of the candlestick. Measure 1¼" up from the bottom of that candle cup, then lightly draw a wavy pencil line at that point—around the circumference. Then draw another wavy light line ¼" below the first.

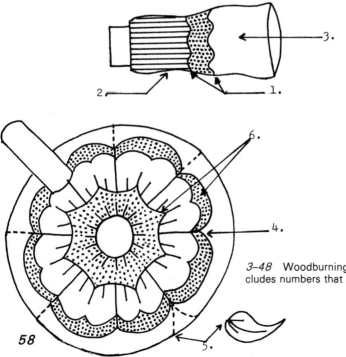

3-48 Woodburning guide for candlestick includes numbers that correspond to directions.

2. Hold the candle cup with pliers while you *line* burn 1" strokes from the bottom of the candle cup up to the bottom wavy line. Lightly *shade* burn all the candle cup up to the 1¼" line.

3. Paint the top of the candle cup with your choice of acrylic color. In our case, it was light blue.

4. Now you may want to trace the pattern, but please try drawing it right on the wood. You can easily measure out the petal spaces (divide the base circumference into eight equal sections) and fill in the rest of the detail with light penciled lines.

5. Draw a leaf (see suggested shape on drawing) on the side of the base at areas indicated by dotted lines on the drawing.

6. *Line* and *dash* burn all lines indicated by solid lines on base in drawing. Lightly *shade* burn the center section (dotted area on drawing) and darkly *shade* burn the outer edges of the flower petals.

7. Being careful to stay within the burned lines, paint the unshaded section of each flower petal yellow, the leaves green, and the background blue (or any color of your choice). In this project you will want to use acrylic paint as it comes from the jar, not thinned to a stain as we have done in other projects.

Grain of Sand Quote

3-49 Woodburning can be combined with simple decoupage.

It would be difficult to estimate how many handcrafters have been or are decoupage artists. To some of these decoupage enthusiasts, wood-burning can add another attractive accent to some of their projects.

On this grain of sand plaque (so named because of the quote on it), the stylized wild flower was burned and the plaque painted before the parchment quote was glued in position. You will note that only the basic outline of that flower is given in the pattern. It is left up to you to adjust the size, use shading, dots, dashes, and line burn strokes to embellish the flower according to your own desires.

Though just the tones of the wood and burning would have been attractive with this parchment quote, we painted the entire background of the plaque, except on the flower (*after* the burning was accomplished and rubbed down), to illustrate a technique. The background and the

3–50 A basic outline pattern for a wild flower.

little shading of color on the flower itself look muted because the entire plaque was antiqued.

When do you apply antiquing glaze? Wait until after you have applied and dried the first two coats of wood finish. Then wipe on the antiquing glaze. Let it set a few minutes and then wipe off as much or as little of it as you desire to give the whole plaque the patina of age.

When you are decoupaging a quote or print onto a wooden surface (which has been woodburned), you can expect to have to apply a few more coats of finish than normally. However, if you apply two coats, sand lightly when dry, apply two more, and so on; you will be surprised how soon you can build up enough depth of this fast-drying finish so that you cannot feel the rough edges of the quote. It is not necessary to completely submerge the woodburned lines, but it is possible if you want that.

Cheese Board

3–51 A cheese board, decorated with a combination of woodburning and decorative painting.

Beginner books for country carvers and tole and decorative painters often contain designs that you can readily adapt to woodburning. In the designs intended for bas-relief carving, the heavy woodburned lines can take the place of "gouged" lines. The rich brown outlines and accents of woodburning onto a presketched tole design on a wooden surface will add definition to painted areas.

On this pictured example, the simple fruit design was rather small for the size of the plaque that I intended to use as a cheese cutting board. A ½" border of dark *plane shading* around the edge, encircled by a narrow band of leaf green color, served to use up the extra space without detracting too much from the center design.

When you are finishing an item that will need to be washed frequently, such as this cheese board, be sure to apply a wood finish that is water resistant. Finish both the front and back sides of the object. Even then it is not a good idea to let such wooden pieces soak in dishwater or be washed in a dishwasher.

In Memory of the One-Room Schoolhouse

In my own country kitchen, one entire wall is hung full of what some people might call bric-a-brac. Actually, almost every object there is hand-made and represents a memory of some time or event in our past life. One day I realized there was no memento on that wall to remind us of my brief career as a country schoolteacher (over thirty-five years ago). Are you old enough to remember the one-room schoolhouse where there might be twenty-one pupils in all eight grades?

Some friends of ours, Delores and Glenn Clauss, manufacture and distribute to craft supply shops an inexpensive line of miniature doll-

3–52   In memory of the one-room schoolhouse of yester-
year.

houses and furniture. One of their smaller houses was just right to create
a schoolhouse to hang on my memory wall. But the school in which I
taught was not the traditional red schoolhouse in that its outside walls
were made of warm brown, large cinder blocks. Here is where the
woodburning technique came in!

   If you would like to use woodburning to help you finish a diorama or
dollhouse in a unique way, here are the steps I followed that should give
you some ideas to use on your project. Horizontal lines (½" apart) were
drawn and *line* burned on both outside walls, continuing around on the
front edges. (Please glance at the picture from time to time, as you read,
and you will easily follow my steps.) Alternate vertical lines (sketched
and burned 1½" apart) connected the horizontal lines and gave the
illusion of large, rectangular cinder blocks. Dark shading, burned over all
the blocks, completed that illusion.

   What about the roof? Tiny, little individual "shake" shingles are available in shops that specialize in miniature supplies. Each shingle was held
firmly with a tweezer on a nonflammable surface as the hot pen was
used to shade it realistically. Even the edges were shaded before each
shingle was glued in place on the roof. This gluing process started on
the bottom row at each side of the roof so that each new row over-

lapped the previous row. A few touches of woodburning disguised a block of wood into a decorative chimney reminiscent of the one that perched above the peak of that old schoolhouse I sought to remember.

Memory also dictated woodburning the wainscoting on the first-floor walls, the rug on the floor, and the trim around the roof. The two evenings spent on this project started me on another hobby—personalizing and antiquing miniature furniture with woodburning. I suppose I am saving these pieces for a dollhouse for the granddaughter I do not have yet.

3–53 Examples of miniature furniture, antiqued and decorated with woodburning.

Customized Toys

Just for fun and to give you another idea of how you could use your woodburning pen, I included these two little wooden cars. Actually, I have used woodburning to safely decorate many unfinished wooden toys for my small grandsons. However, have you ever tried to convince a one-year-old and a four-year-old—by mail—that they should let Grandmother take back some of their favorite toys so she could photograph them for a book? Finally, it seemed easier to buy two new unfinished wooden cars and woodburn them!

On the particular toys pictured, you will notice the wood has a "wild" figure, which would make delicate designs difficult to accomplish. *Flat plane shading* and darkly burned lines completed the decoration of the little car, while *rod* burns gave a "groovy" look to the 500 racer.

On children's toys you will seldom need or want to develop a great depth of wood finish, but you will want to apply one or more coats of a clear finish. Check the label to see that the finish is nontoxic because small children may decide to chew on that toy later.

3-54   A wooden toy Volks was customized with woodburning.

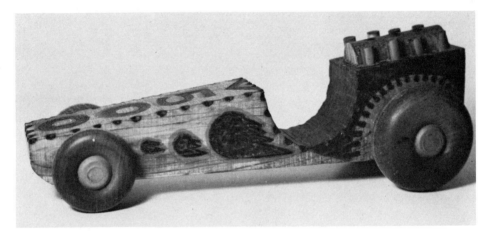

3-55   Or do you prefer an Indianapolis 500 racer?

Little Touches of Woodburning

You can instruct five different people to use their woodburning tool to add some accents to a workshop project and they will each do something different. The weathered alderwood plaques pictured all had a paper veneer sun motif glued in position when the crafters were instructed to use their woodburning pens on them. (Later these plaques were finished to submerge the sunburst design.) As you can see, even the two plaques that both have *rod* burns around their edges are slightly different. One has *dash* burns around the sun's face while the other has *dots* burned in the same location.

Notice how the figure on the other two plaques inspired the wood-burned touches. How would you have used your burn strokes to accent these plaques? You could outline the sun's rays with woodburned lines,

3–56 Little touches of woodburning provide interest.

shade the outer area of the background or around the rays of the sun. You will see other possibilities as you study the picture.

Even when you are making a project using someone else's basic design, nothing says you cannot add your own woodburned touches to make yours uniquely different!

Woodburning can add an accent to quickie craft projects that you may be making for little personal gifts. It adds interest to some craft

3–57 Smile, you are on your way to becoming a woodburner.

activities for groups of teen-agers. A woodburned crescent hanging on a woven strip makes a practical bookmark. Macramé, combined with woodburned rings, creates a fashionwise belt for a slim waist. It takes just a matter of minutes to measure and woodburn a stylized flower on a walnut round. Walnut rounds, already cut and ready to burn, are available in varying sizes at craft supply shops, as are the wooden beads used to accent the alternate half-hitch chain and the child's bracelet. Tiny eyelet screws can be attached to any piece of woodburned wood to make it easy to incorporate it into macramé, weaving, and jewelry.

Most of this is accomplished by just measuring and marking reference points on the object, then freehand burning, using the basic burn strokes. However, if you still want to "trace and burn," the next chapter is for you.

3–58 Visual suggestions for quickie woodburning projects for yourself or for young people's group activities.

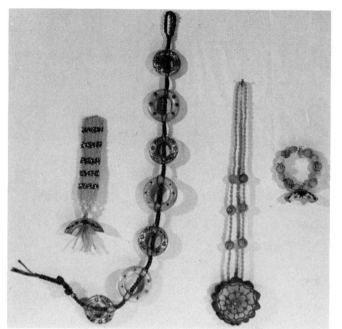

4 MORE PATTERNS

4-1 Imagine the sun is shining down on this dove of peace and then add burned shadows in the appropriate areas if you decide to woodburn this pattern.

4-2 Burned on weathered wood and highlighted with acrylics, this still life would be suitable to hang in a country kitchen.

More Patterns

Because most small how-to books include lots of patterns, I did not want those of you who like to use them to be slighted in this book. There are twelve patterns in this chapter, varied in both their intended use and in the skill required to woodburn them. Naturally, the easiest ones are shown first.

Suggestions in the captions are given as to how each pattern can be used, but do not let that stifle your own creativity. Add your own touches and use them as you deem appropriate. You may also find that, after reading the rest of the book, you will gain new ideas about adaptations or uses you can make of these patterns.

When tracing patterns on wood, remember to use graphite tracing paper, rather than ordinary carbon, to avoid smudges. And after woodburning is completed, remove any visible traced lines or marks with an eraser or very fine sandpaper before proceeding with the finishing.

4–3   A basic outline that will need your woodburned shading or light line strokes to add the fluffy appearance.

4–4 Look at designs on linoleum or floor tile. They can inspire ideas like this one motif that was designed for the lid top of a round basket purse.

4–5 Alderwood rings can be decorated with woodburning to make unique mini-frames.

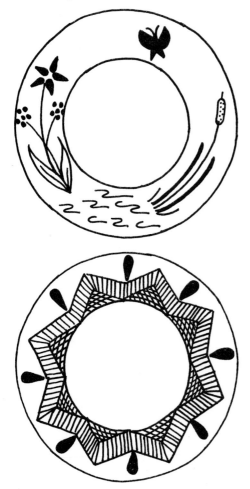

4–6 Some visual suggestions for varying the shape and the woodburned decoration of the ever popular mushroom motif.

4-7 Do you recognize this simple drawing as illustrating the theme of an old song, "Tie a yellow ribbon 'round the old oak tree"? Why not burn a valentine on a shingle and add the appropriate words to convey your own personal message?

4-8 An antique picture frame, hanging in a shop, inspired this design for a 7" X 9" plaque (can be reduced for 5" X 7"). A photograph, appropriate quote, or print could be decoupaged in the oval center.

4-9 A pattern for a repeat border design that can be used full size (repeat measurements—3" wide X 8½") on large areas or reduced one half (1½" X 4¼") for a smaller border. Adjustment in length measurement can be made where the dotted lines appear on the drawing. For more information on repeat borders, see chapter 6.

4-10 A pattern for an entwined grapevine to be woodburned on an arte frame.

4-11 Lisa Petranoff designed this Osprey as a companion to the Black Duck in chapter 3. Practice woodburning a while before you attempt to use this or the next pattern.

4-12 A companion for Pharaoh (chapter 3) was also designed by Lisa Petranoff. When you seek to woodburn this lady, choose a plaque that has an even texture and subtle figure.

PART TWO

AFTER PRACTICE, YOU'RE READY

5 PLAN YOUR OWN WOODBURNING DESIGNS

Now banish your negative attitude. Who says you cannot design? If you are expecting a textbook discussion at this point or a set of rules that will teach you to design, you will be disappointed. In my teaching experience it is difficult enough to inspire confidence in beginner crafters (to try designing for themselves) without hampering them with a hard and fast set of rules to follow.

Years ago, I gained confidence from John Kenny when I studied his book *Ceramic Design*. Since then I have ascribed to the theory that there are no set rules in art, design being mostly a matter of personal judgment, reflecting one's own experience and taste as well as one's skill. There is no way that anyone could guarantee that your ideas of good or bad design would match mine, and who is to say which of us is right? Naturally, as you experiment and practice woodburning, your designs should improve and become easier to execute. You may even find that your own ideas of good or bad design will change as you first practice using other people's designs; second, research through books and magazines or visit arts and crafts shops and galleries to glean ideas that you can adopt to your own use; finally, persevere in your attempts to design yourself and become a better woodburner.

Practice projects, pictured methods, drawings, and information about certain elements (how to compensate for lack of sketching ability, how to make use of the figure of the wood, and the like) included here should be helpful to you. Certainly, it will be encouraging.

Of course, if you later become involved in selling or entering your woodburned works in arts and crafts juried competitions, you will be subject to the individual judge's or customer's comprehension of design. However, at this beginning point, the only person you have to please is yourself.

Block Candle Holders

5-1   Woodburned block candle holders are a practice exercise in designing and woodburning.

You see two candle holders pictured here. I see a practice project that incorporates the use of negative and positive shading. It will also demonstrate to you how much a beginning woodburner, who wants to create his/her own designs, can accomplish by just using geometric shapes, such as those featured here. Such designs can be executed to achieve a very modern look.

Using the identical geometric design, but shading different portions in alternate areas, makes an obvious difference as you can see in the pictures and drawings. When the outer areas are darkly shaded, do you notice the design appears to be larger? Interesting borders can be designed, using just such simple geometric, identical shapes in a row, while alternating the shaded areas.

There are various ways in which you can vary the shading itself. On these candle holders *flat plane shading* strokes produced a very dark coloring. Lighter, *mottled shading,* if used, would be more delicate and provide less contrast. Or you could shade the areas desired with burned

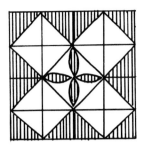
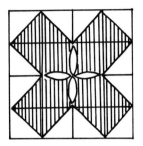

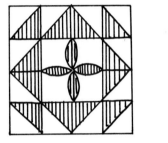

5–2 Negative and positive shading on geometric figures.

dots (which would also develop more texture) or use multiple lines. The closer the lines or dots are spaced and burned, the darker the appearance of the shading (see drawing 5–3).

You can practice this use of geometric figures with negative and positive shading on any piece of wood. If you should want to make block candle holders like these, here are a few practical suggestions.

5–3 Repeated lines or dots can be used in woodburning to develop different depths of shading tones.

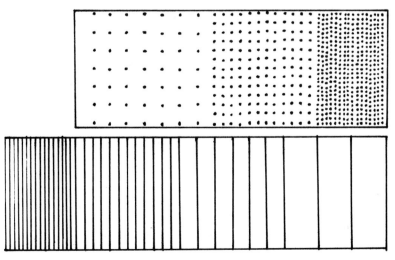
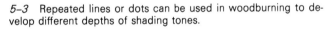

A sturdy, solid block of wood (3⅞" x 3⅞" x 3½") was tooled around the top edge. This made a slight curved slope on that edge from the center where the 2" diameter candle will stand. The candle is held in position on the holder by a thin 3" long nail that was pounded into the center of the top. If the nail has a big head, you must clip it off with a wire cutter, once the nail is in the wood. When the candle holder is woodburned and finished, you can impale the candle on the headless nail for stability.

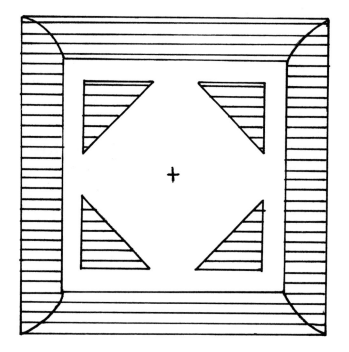

5–4   Suggested pattern design for top of candle holders.

Smaller blocks of wood can be equally effective as candle holders if you use appropriate size candles. The top edge tooling on the block is not absolutely necessary, but thorough sanding of the entire block before woodburning is. When the woodburning and finishing are done, glue a felt square to the bottom of the candle holder if you want to protect the surface on which it will sit.

Why don't you try designing a geometric-shape border for around each side of the block, leaving the natural wood grain showing in the center? Then you could probably use a candle of a larger diameter because the block candle holder would appear to be larger with that design.

5-5 Sailboat by Regina Petrutis
How important shading becomes in many woodburned scenes is obvious in this woodburned design by Regina. Do not become a slave to the habit of always darkly burning everything in the center design, while leaving all the background unburned. Think of how this sail and these birds loom out of the dark, vertically shaded background. Just as real waves are not all the same color, the horizontal shading of these waves produced varied shades of brown.

Just Lines

Sometimes all you need to make up a design is lines. When you are seeking something different in framing miniatures, collections of small jewelry, foreign coins, stamps, pressed flowers, and snapshots, there is almost no end to the possibilities of how simple, straight, woodburned lines can enhance these small objects. Pictured is a part of a coin collection. The mounted coins are not particularly valuable, but the sentimental value to the owner is great because of the year these coins were minted. Each plaque has a different background and shows just a few of the combinations of straight, burned lines that can be used for effective background design. Normally, you will find these background designs are more suitable for plaques that have a more formal look and that do not have distressed or irregular edges.

There are several vital points to remember when executing this type of design. Experiment on squared paper with your ruler and pencil until you have selected the combination of lines that you want to burn. Decide which areas you are going to shade, if any. After the plaque is sanded, *accurately* measure and lightly pencil mark each line of your

5-6

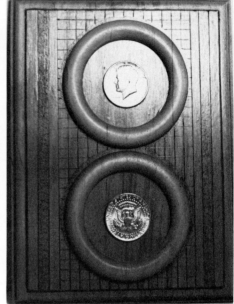

5-7

5-8

A coin collection mounted on plaques that were decorated with different combinations of straight woodburned lines and a little shading.

5-9

5-10

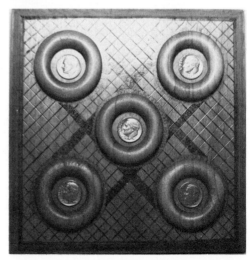

design on the wood. Do not press too hard on the pencil because you do not want to dent the wood and make marks that cannot be erased if need be.

Diagonal, squared, or grillwork lines are all burned easily by using a metal edge ruler as a guide for the point edge as it burns each line. Use a consistent, medium pressure as you draw the hot pen point steadily toward you along the metal ruler edge. Hold the ruler firmly in position. Be sure the pen point edge is held at a right angle to the wood, so it does not slant to one or the other side and allow the flat plane to touch the wood.

If you wish the burned line to be darker, burn over it again. When burning a line across others already burned, avoid letting the previously burned line deflect the pen point edge from your intended burning direction along the metal edge.

It is easier to finish the plaque completely and apply several coats of wood finish to the flat back rings separately before you glue them together. The object to be enclosed by the ring should be attached last.

If you wish to permanently seal the object in the ring on the plaque, ask your craft supply retailer about clear coating resin that can be used for that purpose. In your search for design possibilities, do not ever overlook using simple combinations of just straight lines.

5-11 Combinations of lines can become the background for some woodburned designs when you are not particularly striving for realism.

Two Floral Oval Plaques

Part of the decision you must make, when planning a woodburned design, is whether your ultimate finished project will be served best by just using the wood tone colors of the natural or stained wood for the background to the varied brown shades of your woodburning. Or do you want to introduce other color accents by using paint on certain areas after the woodburning is finished? There is no hard and fast rule that dictates what you should do. You are free to suit your own taste, and what fun it is to experiment and develop your own creativity.

5-12   5-13

Compare the two floral oval plaques. One has natural wood background while the other background is painted.

When a delicate wild flower is woodburned in an alderwood oval, such as the one pictured, the figure of the wood is subtle and detracts nothing from the woodburned flower, so it would be highly unlikely that you would want to paint it. However, the use of some color on the rim of the plaque serves to better frame the flower and focus attention on it, that is, if the paint's color is subtle enough to avoid overwhelming the center panel.

If you look at the rose plaque pictured, you will see another possibility. You can use the figure of the natural wood within the burned lines on the flower while the background and frame are painted. Incidentally, if you cannot sketch flowers, you will be able to find suitable patterns in craft magazines, embroidery transfers, decorative painting books, and so on. Why not try adding your own touches to those copied designs even when you do use them?

By this stage in your woodburning experience, you do not need anyone to hold your hand and guide you through each specific, separate step of a project. Hopefully, you have learned to just let these projects trigger your own ideas and have begun to branch out on your own. For a few pages let us explore the possibilities of using woodburned designs to suggest certain themes.

At times the object on which you are going to woodburn—its grain, figure, or color—may suggest or even dictate a design idea to you. Other times, the shape of the piece itself is the inspiration. But, occasionally, you will want to specifically achieve a certain mood or feeling with your design because of the way the object is going to be used or how it will fit in with your decor.

How do you go about creating a design on an item that will convey the mood or feeling you desire? A majority of handcrafters may not be able to call on their own picture memories and then automatically sketch just what they want. Aren't the ones who can lucky? For the rest of us, once you have decided on the basic theme, look for drawings and pictures—not to copy, but for inspiration—in magazines and books. Check the other furnishings in your room, even the wallpaper that might echo the theme. Look for simple motifs that you might incorporate into a design that would suggest your theme.

South Seas Napkin Holder

5-14   Recognize the South Seas theme?

In the pictured example the attempt was to relate to a tropical South Seas feeling that already existed in a breakfast room. In my brief research, it seemed bamboo, lush undergrowth, and airy insects appeared in many South Seas pictures (plus beautiful bathing beauties that I could not hope to draw), so they became the components for the design.

You must always take into consideration the shape of the wooden item upon which the design is to be used. When it is a three-dimensional object like this napkin holder, do not just burn a center design on each side and call it done. Try to plan so the whole piece will be unified in the design and present interesting aspects from any viewing angle.

On the napkin holder, the mottled shading on all the edges provide bordering that will not detract from the front or back, which give limited glimpses of lush growth. Though the napkins (or letters, if you decide to use this project as a letter holder instead) usually conceal the interior, you will note by the drawings there is an airy grillwork burned there anyway to complete the whole.

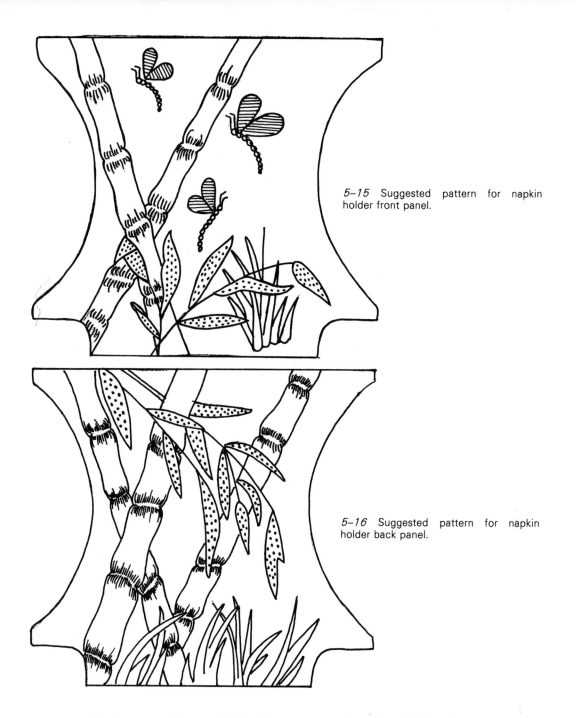

5–15 Suggested pattern for napkin holder front panel.

5–16 Suggested pattern for napkin holder back panel.

By the way, this napkin holder was purchased unfinished and knocked down from a craft supply shop. Three-dimensional objects are always easiest to burn if that can be done before the parts are glued or nailed together. It makes it easier to hold the woodburning pen at a right angle and move the piece around as you burn.

If the theme design you desire can be drawn or painted with lines and shading, it can be duplicated in rich, brown woodburning. Plus, designs need not always be very intricate or complicated to convey a mood or feeling.

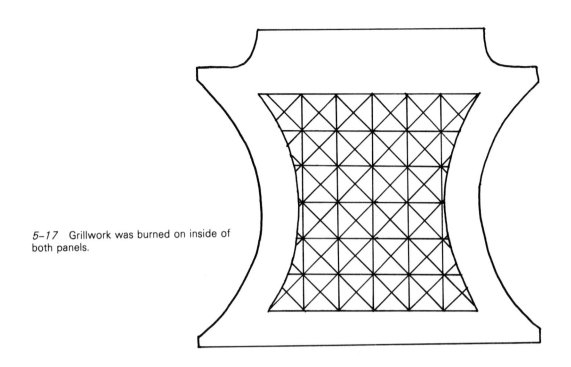

5-17 Grillwork was burned on inside of both panels.

5-18 Shading and diamonds completed the decoration of the handle and base.

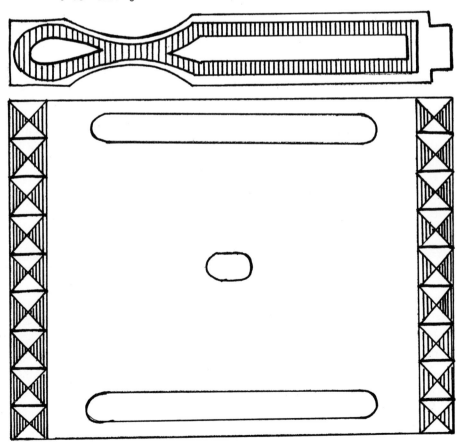

Pennsylvania Dutch Designs

5-19 Hex signs are said to bring good luck wherever they are found.

These are easy to adapt, and it is probable that no designs are more suggestive of Pennsylvania Dutch folk art than their hex signs. From the primitive, simple, circular hex signs that appeared on barn walls in the early days to the more intricately patterned ones that decorate the walls of commercial restaurants and gift shops today, the basic folk art of the hex signs has pretty much remained intact. Hearts, flowers, leaves, birds, and geometric figures are combined in a variety of designs. Usually, bright primary colors are used to paint them, and the addition of dark brown woodburned outlines increases the clean-cut strength of the hex designs.

Before tackling a major project, such as burning a band of hex designs on the sides of an unfinished chest of drawers, try this simple project for practice. Why not buy a package of plain cork coasters or some round, thin basswood plaques and make a set of coasters with a different hex design burned on each? You can start with the simple patterns given here.

Basic patterns for simple hex signs to woodburn.

5-20   5-21   5-22

Then look through Pennsylvania Dutch folk art books in your library or local craft supply shop for more pattern ideas. Do not overlook those little cocktail napkins, sold in almost every gift shop, that have borders of hex designs.

Practicing on hex designs first will usually give you the inspiration to go on to burning larger designs of Pennsylvania Dutch origin. Can't you just see that unfinished chest of drawers with a burned hex sign behind each drawer pull, a band of hex signs down each side, and a larger design burned over the top? With the proper finish over them, these designs will stand the wear and tear of normal usage for years.

Memory Box for Egyptian Treasures

Did I achieve my desired effect of transforming this ready-made memory box into an appropriate receptacle for souvenirs of a rewarding trip to a museum displaying Egyptian treasures? Truthfully, I was not completely satisfied with the results, but decided to use the project anyway to illustrate for you how anyone can create a theme design.

After research through some books and a trip to the museum, the motifs that related to an Egyptian theme that I could incorporate into a woodburned design seemed to be mosaic tiles, snakes, and tapestry. On something of a different shape and purpose, it might have been pyra-

5–23 Miniature replicas of King Tut's treasures will be displayed in this woodburned memory box.

5–24 Different textures, shades of color, and motifs can all be accomplished with the woodburning pen.

mids or animals that would serve the purpose. Remember when you are seeking to create a theme design—if you are handicapped by a lack of drawing talent—you can use tracing paper to copy motifs from magazines or books for your own use. Due to copyright laws, I could not do this and reproduce those designs for your use in this book.

The effect of woven tapestry in the back of the box was achieved by just mottle shading the pencil-sketched outline of the pseudo-woven blocks. The outline was not line burned because that would have detracted from the fabric texture feeling. Once the snake and jeweled armband motifs were outline burned on the sides, large block tiles were outlined around them. Alternate mottle-shaded blocks were bordered by dark shading bands that framed the motifs and contributed an aged look.

Closely spaced, burned dots on the back of the snake and on the armband provided shading that varied from the great deal of mottled shading that had already been used. The wood from which this memory box was made was very soft. Because slightly more pressure was used than usual when burning the shading, it was easy to produce a rougher texture on the surface that also "aged" the box.

Native American Folk Art

Indians were the natives of our country when the white man came, and they had already originated a wealth of primitive design for us. The brown tones of woodburning have a natural affinity for these designs and they can be kept simple enough to encourage even the beginner to use them. So let us think about where we could find some of these designs—not to copy, but to look at for inspiration. Stop at your local library. Magazines, reference and children's books may be your answer, though greeting cards with Hopi Indian illustrations on them were the inspiration for the Eye of God weaving that I chose to make and include here. (If my children were small again, I would be tempted to finish a set of bedroom furniture with woodburned Indian designs.)

In case you would like to duplicate this Eye of God weaving, or adapt it to your own design, here are a few notes on procedure and some drawings.

Materials
1 8" x 10" metal wire frame (W. T. Rogers)
1 6½" outside diameter, unfinished wooden ring
1 2¾" outside diameter, unfinished wooden ring
2 2" base, unfinished spandrels (Woodring Craft)
wood finish, fast drying and clear
Quick 'n Easy Weaving Kit (Stanley Berroco) brown tones
    Homespun—50% wool, 50% nylon
    Dji Dji—77% wool, 23% viscose

5-25 Weaving, woodburning, and a little macramé combine to make this Eye of God.

Nubs 'n Slubs—80% wool, 20% viscose
Ove Linda—95% wool, 5% nylon
orange acrylic jute, approximately 30 yards (Unicraft Products)
miscellaneous: white craft glue that dries clear and flexible, scissors,
  ruler, pyrolectric pen, cloth tape measure

Procedure: It is practical to do the woodburning first so the finish coats can be drying while you are weaving the background. Of course, you will finish the rings and double spandrel with wood finish as in the general directions.

Woodburning

1. Center double spandrel, Eye of God. Remember making Christmas ornaments of the spandrels earlier in chapter 3? Then look at drawing 5–26 and you will see how the rod and line burn strokes are used to burn this simple design.

2. Hanger ring. Sand the ring well before you start burning. Do not try to trace the design on the ring from the drawing. Measure reference points and draw right on the wood (see drawing 5–27). Measuring and burning on a rounded ring is slightly more difficult than working on a flat surface. Use a cloth tape measure that will wrap around the curve rather than a straight ruler for measuring.

3. Large, encircling ring (see drawing 5–28). Where the pattern seems to go beyond the sides of the ring, it indicates areas where the design will wrap around the ring. Do not be afraid to sketch the designs

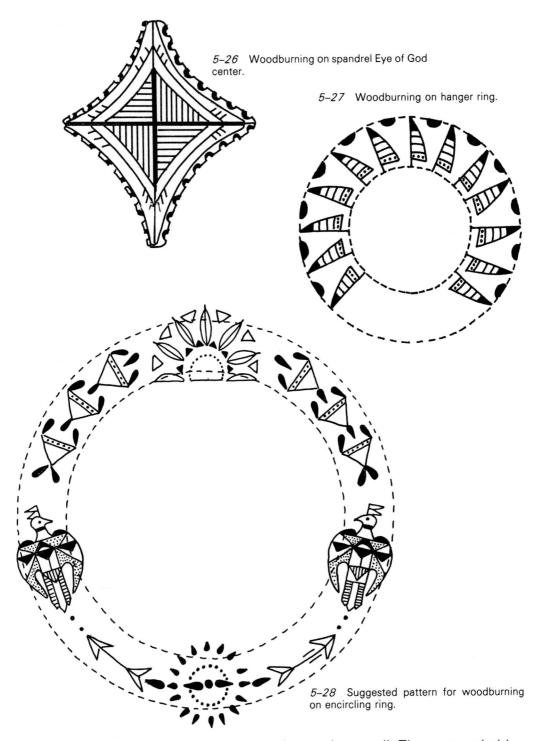

5-26 Woodburning on spandrel Eye of God center.

5-27 Woodburning on hanger ring.

5-28 Suggested pattern for woodburning on encircling ring.

on the ring freehand even if you do not draw well. These are primitive symbols and do not require a lot of artistic skill to duplicate.

By the way, the symbols on the ring are supposed to tell a story. Can you decipher it? An important chief (see the headdress symbol at the top) went on a two-day hunt (symbol at bottom) and killed (arrows) two large eagles and six deer. Successful hunt under the Eye of God.

90

Weaving

1. See drawing 5–29.

a. Cut six cords of orange acrylic jute, each 28" long. Cut seven orange cords, each 36" long. Double each cord in half and attach each to the top of the metal ring frame with a lark's head knot. Alternate

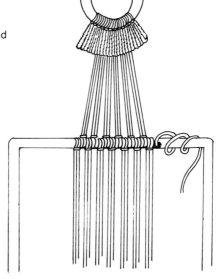

5–29 Attaching warp cords to hanger ring and wire frame with macramé knots.

attaching a longer cord (36" doubled = 18") and then a shorter (28" doubled = 14"), etc. Longer cords should be on each side.

b. Pull the shorter cords up from the frame and attach each to the hanger ring with reverse half hitch, leaving approximately 5" between the hanger ring and frame. Trim (approximately 3") and fringe the ends and comb them down from the ring.

c. Pull the longer cords down and attach each to the bottom of the metal wire frame with a double half hitch. These fourteen cords in the middle of the frame will be the warp cords for your weaving.

d. Attach the end of a piece of brown weft to the top of the wire frame with glue (beside the knotted warp cords) and wrap snugly around all the bare areas of the frame.

2. See drawing 5–30, page 92.

a. Weave 2½" down the frame (over two cords, under two warp cords), using any of the novelty cords you prefer. The strands on the drawing are not pushed tightly together, but you will "beat" the weft cords tight enough so that the orange warp will not show.

b. Use seven yards of orange acrylic jute to weave a center panel 4½" long over the center twelve warp cords only, not the frame. Pull the weft cords tighter toward the center to create curve.

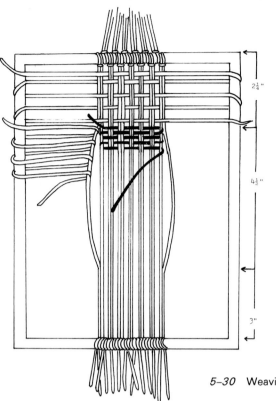

5-30 Weaving steps for background for Eye of God.

c. Use the two outside warp cords and weave side panels of brown tone novelty yarn between that card and frame edge. These will also be 4½" long.

d. Weave clear across frame and warp cords (back to under two, over two) for 3", which should bring you to the bottom of the frame. Conceal the ends of your weaving cords within the weaving, after dotting them with glue.

3. You now have fourteen cord ends hanging down from the metal frame. Tie a square knot in the first four cords. Repeat on next three cords, again on next three cords, and finally on four remaining cord ends. Comb and fringe the acrylic jute ends and trim them to an even length.

Glue the double spandrel Eye of God over the center orange panel of weaving. Glue the large encircling ring on top of weaving around the Eye of God.

How Is the Figure?

At this point we are concerned not with your figure but with that of the figure that appears on the plaque you are planning to woodburn. As you will remember from chapter 1, the figure is a natural design, or pattern, that you can see on the cut surface of a piece of wood. The grain is only one part of the elements that developed that figure on that wood.

A very strong, obvious figure on any piece of wood used for wood-burning is bound to influence the final appearance of the woodburned design on it. Your objective should be to plan so the figure on the wood will enhance or add to your design, rather than to detract from it. Small, very intricate designs will not only be more difficult to burn on such highly patterned surfaces (which are apt to have wide variations between the darker lines of summerwood and springwood), but will also have a tendency to get lost in the figure itself.

This is definitely not to imply that strongly figured woods are to be avoided. It means rather that strong, relatively simple, woodburned designs on them are more apt to dominate the natural figure than vice versa. Heavier lines, dark shading, and positive images are dominating features in a woodburned design.

The figure of the wood can be incorporated into a part of the final design. Look at the fat, ready-to-be-caught fish pictured here and in the drawing of the pattern. Note how the natural figure on the redwood plaque suggests the movement of water around the fish and also the appearance of scales and lines on the fish's body. But the same figure could suggest other possibilities with other designs. If you had wood-burned a group of mushrooms or a bird on this plaque, the same figure or pattern on the wood might suggest tree trunks. Or turn the plaque around, ignoring the fish on it in the picture, and you can probably see how the natural figure suggests a seashore on which you could burn a scene of shells, vegetation, sailboat, and so on.

If you wish to trace and woodburn Lisa Petranoff's fish pattern given here, you do not have to go into a craft supply shop and search through the redwood plaques until you find one with an identical figure. You can

5–31 The woodburned fish and foliage, the strong figure on the wooden plaque, and the shape of that plaque are all component parts of the finished design.

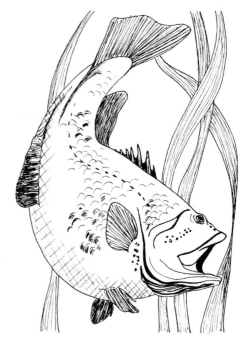

5–32 Pattern designed by Lisa Petranoff.

duplicate nearly the same effect on almost any strongly figured wood with some vertical lines. The pretooled and stained edges on the plaque picture were executed by the manufacturer, but you can choose a plaque without these features if you desire.

If, as sometimes happens, you have woodburned the design on the wood and it does not stand out from the figure as much as you desire, there is a solution. Use a thinned, acrylic wood stain (slightly darker than the redwood) to stain the fish. This will darken and emphasize the fish but not detract from the woodburning and still allow the figure to show through and add lines to the fish's body. In the plaque pictured, a transparent, very light green stain was also wiped on the "underwater" leaves.

Before you start woodburning on any strongly figured plaque, try to envision your design on that wood and gauge what the figure will do to the overall finished appearance of your project. Plan a positive use of the lines and patterns of the figure. Do not ignore it because it will be part of your design on that plaque when you are finished.

Beginners' Bracelets

Wide-band, alderwood bracelets are excellent projects for beginning woodburners who would like to try their hand at freehand burning. The way these alderwood bracelets are cut develops a figure that is attractive, when finished, and gives even the simplest of woodburned designs a natural beauty. The trick is not to cover too much of that figure with the woodburning and use a light touch.

Two distinctive wide-band bracelet designs are sketched here. They are not necessarily for you to copy but rather to give you ideas to spur your own designs. After all, the grain and figure on the unfinished band you have to woodburn may suggest an entirely different design than these. Certainly, the one here (whose design suggests a desert scene) would be nothing without that figure of the wood behind it.

Try to identify which burn strokes were used and where on these designs. If you have practiced the dash, dot, line, and petal burn strokes, you will find it easy to burn these or similar designs on the bracelets. In chapter 8 you will have the opportunity to see how an artist burns bracelets.

5-33 Beginner's bracelets combine simple woodburned design with natural beauty of alderwood figure and soft gleam of a smooth wood finish.

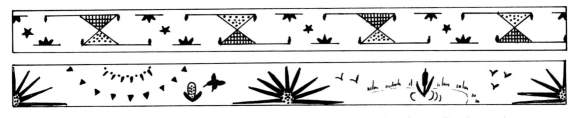

5-34 Sketches of bracelet designs, detailing the use of beginner's woodburning strokes.

Tranquil Shore

A receding tide, leaving whirled patterns in the sand of the beach, peaceful rolling hills in the distance, and shimmering water, swirling up to the beach, are all there. And they were there (including the difference in the color of the water) on this plaque before it was ever touched by the few woodburned lines and shaded areas that I used to reinforce the scenic impression. So I cannot take much credit for creating this plaque, but just for recognizing its possibilities and finishing it.

To develop more sheen and highlight the lighter colored "water" area, a gloss wood finish was applied there while semigloss finish was used on the rest of the plaque.

No, you do not have much chance of finding a plaque figured exactly like this one so you can duplicate this scene. But that isn't really what you want. You want to find a scene of your own. Surprisingly enough, by just keeping your eyes open (when you examine plaques and pieces of wood for your other projects), you will often turn up very similar ones that have unique design possibilities and require very little additional woodburning on your part to complete them. It is not always the complexity of the design that determines its effectiveness.

5-35 A Tranquil Shore

5-36 Just following the swirly lines of the figure on the wooden shoe is all that is necessary to develop a pleasing pattern to decorate this hanging plant holder.

A "Wild Figure" Sign

A small sign was needed to hang in the back window of our mini motor home to proclaim our CB numbers. Since my pyrolectric pen was handy, naturally the numbers were woodburned on this little pine sign. However, the plain reverse side, which was visible from the interior of the motor home, did not please me. So one day at a picnic table in a camping site, I woodburned the design you see pictured.

By the way, woodburning is one craft that is easy to take along on a vacation. All you really need to pack is the pen, sandpaper, and a piece of wood. Find an electrical outlet when you get to your destination, and

5-37 This is often called a "wild figure" since it is very obvious and there is a great variance between springwood and summerwood in color and hardness.

start woodburning. Many a rainy day in a camper or in a fishing resort cabin can be a great time for crafting for you or the children. You can do the wood finishing on your projects when you get back home.

The figure on this wooden sign was "wild" and suggested the movement of a strong wind to me. So it was left exposed and now "blows" the words (Mini-B is our grandson's nickname for our mini motor home) and the tangles of flowers and leaves that were burned on it. Touches of acrylic color were added to the flowers to prevent the "wind" figure from overcoming the burned lines of the floral border.

Simple, floral borders (see pattern 5–38) are effective where a quote is decoupaged on the plaque (in place of the words Mini-B). As always, when burning on such an obvious figure, be prepared to adjust your pressure on the woodburning pen. It will burn quickly and deeply on the softer, lighter springwood, while additional pressure and time will be required to burn the same size line on the darker bands of summerwood.

5–38 A floral border pattern that you might want to adapt to a decoupaged quote.

Wood-grained Sunflowers

No, it wasn't an accident that the edges of the plaque were cut off in this picture of the sunflower. It was an attempt to get as close as possible to the flower to better enable you to see how the natural figure of the wood provided the interior lines and shading within the woodburned lines of the sunflower petals.

As you can judge by the strong figure revealed on the petals of the sunflowers, the rest of the plaque was just as busy. It would have been difficult to make the woodburned flowers as dominant as they are if they had had to "fight" with such obvious figure detail all around them. The solution was to take full advantage of the figure in the flower blossom areas, while obscuring the rest under several coats of acrylic paint. Certainly, you could have shade burned the entire background or stipple painted it. Neither technique would have provided such sharp, strong contrast that compels the attention to the wood-grained sunflowers.

5-39 A wood-grained sunflower with a solid, acrylic-painted background.

5-40 Basic outline pattern for the wood-grained sunflower.

A Matter of Knots

When you first try burning your own design that is to incorporate the figure of knots or swirly grain appearing on the wood as part of that design, keep it simple. Study the figure on the wood piece first. What form does it suggest to you? If you do not like the first form that comes to mind, keep looking. Turn the plaque around and view it from different angles until another form suggests itself to you.

5–41 A knot becomes a bug who looks at home on a weathered alderwood plaque.

5–42 Is it a cotton boll or a flower? Perhaps neither—it is an exercise in developing creativity.

The bug, pictured on the plaque here, probably came to my mind because I had just uncovered a nest of bugs in a rotten log in our woods. As it was, with the knot as his body, closely spaced petal burns (that followed the lines around the knot) became realistic insect legs. If you turn the picture of that plaque upside down, you can visualize how the knotty hole could have been used as the end of a fallen log. Wild flowers, foliage, a bird, or an animal could have been woodburned on it with the log to create a woodland scene.

Is it a cotton boll or a flower that is pictured on another one of the plaques? I really do not know because I was not trying to realistically portray either. The graceful swirls around the distinctive knot just suggested the direction of the burned lines there. The smaller stem leads the eye through the other expanding swirls to the focus point, while the heavier stem served to repeat the swirl line and give balance to the design.

The person who delights in creating designs with the help of the natural figure (knots, defects, grain, variance in color and texture, and so on) is not the one who complains to the craft supply retailer about the fact that a plaque has those features. Try this exercise in creativity. When you look over the wood pieces that are available for your use, discover whether there isn't an image, scene, or form in your mind that you could translate onto the wood with the aid of your pyrolectric pen.

This weathered alderwood plaque, woodburned by Audronē, was

5-43 Another knot . . . another bug!

5-45 Audronē's Owl, designed and wood-burned by Audronē Bartys. This plaque is owned by Woodring Craft.

5-44 Rather than try to disguise three knots, a long brown streak of decayed wood, and several areas of extreme color variance, they were incorporated into this woodburned backyard scene.

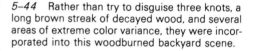

loaned to us by Woodring Craft, Inc., of New York City. It is an excellent example of how an artist contrives to incorporate the figure (including, in this case, knots and grain) on a particular piece of wood until it becomes an integral part of the design. (More of Audronē's woodburning is pictured in chapter 8.)

A close study of the woodburning on this plaque reveals not only the artistic use of the three knots, but also how burn strokes are applied creatively. Notice the small strokes that convey the illusion of soft feathers on the owl, smaller ones on the head and larger ones on the body. The outline of that owl was not starkly divided from the background by a continuous burned line, but was left slightly irregular to further suggest ruffled feathers. No overall mottled shading or straight lines appear on this tree. Each burn stroke was specifically placed to artistically develop the impression of the gnarled bark of a very old tree.

No, we are not suggesting that any nonartist, beginning woodburner could copy this plaque. It is rather an example of the type of woodburning those of you with artistic talent can aspire to when you have learned to make creative use of the figure on the wood and have developed your mastery of various burn strokes.

6 WOODBURNING HOME ACCESSORIES

Woodburning can be used to decorate and finish many pieces of furniture or other accessories that you can use in your home or give as gifts. Once you have developed your skill and confidence, even larger pieces will not daunt your zeal, and you will wield your pyrolectric pen as effectively as you might a paintbrush. Let's look at some examples.

Bookcase Rejuvenated with Woodburning

This little inexpensive set of shelves had been around our house so long (unfinished) that it had been relegated to the basement to hold empty fruit jars. When I was experimenting on Egyptian designs, I decided to woodburn the top of it for practice.

As often happens, when you are practicing, the finished top turned out to be too attractive to junk. But the sides and shelves had collected water stains and ground-in soil over the years. Besides, the wood had faded in some areas and darkened in others. Even a thorough sanding refused to budge some of these defects. Dark, flat plane shaded bands provided accents on the sides, but the overall, mottled shading is what obliterated the remaining defects—inside and out. The only things that the woodburned shading could not disguise were the large knots. Even they were made less obvious.

By planning the position and measurements of the checkerboard tile blocks on the shelves to conceal the water rings, it was possible to leave

6–1 These unfinished storage shelves were rejuvenated with wood-burning and finish.

alternate squares natural. The edges of the shelves were sanded clean so they were left natural as well. Frankly, the checkerboard design on the shelves looked so much like inlaid wood that it drew lots of favorable comments. The same design, woodburned on the top, would have been effective and would have provided more continuity of design on the bookcase.

The things you learn from doing one project usually spur you on to more. So, if you want to make a bookcase similar to this one, here are some things I learned. These inexpensive, unfinished bookshelves are usually unassembled when you purchase them. This is an advantage since it is easier and quicker to sand and woodburn the individual pieces before you nail and/or glue them together. If possible, examine the pieces before you purchase the shelves. Avoid ones that have a lot of large dark knots unless you have plans for a design that incorporates these knots.

Though the shelves pictured have no back, the new ones now available in stores do. Overall, mottled shade burning on such a large area as the back does not take as long as you would think when you can lay the piece flat on your worktable during the burning. A shaded backing on the shelves will focus attention on the pseudo-inlaid design even more.

When the woodburning is completed on all the pieces and the surface has been hand rubbed with a fine finishing pad, glue and nail them together per the manufacturer's instructions. Check the shelves over when assembled and the glue is dry, and retouch any spots that need woodburning and/or sanding. Then apply the wood finish. You may want to put on more coats of finish than usual to develop the high sheen and depth of finish that is desirable on fine furniture.

The appearance and texture of overall, mottle shade burning on furniture sometimes is said to resemble that of leather. It certainly completely disguises and enhances the appearance of inexpensive wood in furniture. It seals and is as permanent as stain and does not chip or crack like paint may under finish.

Can this woodburning technique be used when refinishing old furniture? Only if the piece has been stripped and sanded back to the original wood. Burning on an old finish will produce a gummy mess and is not satisfactory. However, burning over some traces of old stain remaining on the wood can be done. The easiest way is to start with unfinished furniture. It may take longer to complete a woodburned finish on a piece of furniture than to slap on a coat of paint. But think of the conversation piece you will own—like no one else's!

It will be interesting to see if you develop a habit like mine as you become more and more involved in the use of the pyrolectric pen. That is the habit of seldom decorating and finishing the same object twice with the same design. The figure of the wood, the use of the object, a new design idea that you have not tried, all these conspire to keep you from getting bogged down in burning the same design over and over.

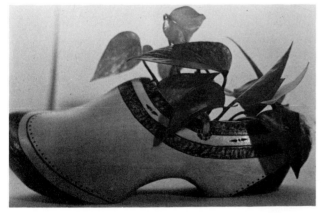

6-2

What a joy it is to have so many design possibilities that seldom will you woodburn the same design twice, even on identical objects.

6-3

Woodburned Bookends

6–4 Woodburning is a quick and easy way to decorate a set of wooden bookends.

The flat back ring, glued in the center of the design, gives these bookends a third dimension, but it is the woodburned design contrast that really gives the clean, modern, and masculine appearance. Since these were made as a gift for my young son-in-law, that was exactly my intention. And since I was in a hurry, I bought an unfinished, presanded, and tooled set of bookends (complete with metal base plates) at a craft supply shop. This same design could easily be used on rectangular pieces of wood (approximately 5" x 4 ¾" x ½" thick) that you could cut yourself. But when you think of cutting the metal base plates, and so on, you can see why it is much easier to buy the packaged unfinished bookend sets. You will also need two flat back rings that are available in craft shops.

Procedure

1. This is another geometric design that you will find easy to measure and draw right on the wood, rather than tracing. If you are burning on different size bookends, you will note that the design will be easy to adapt (see drawing 6–5).

2. *Line* burn all the solid guidelines. Here is where a metal edge ruler for guiding the woodburning pen point will come in handy. Use the *flat plane* burn stroke to shade the dark diagonal bands (shown by diagonal lines on the drawing) and the alternate diamonds (indicated by small squares) above and below the circle.

Mottle shade burn the inside circle (indicated by horizontal lines) and the outside edges of the bookends. Run the rod of the pen quickly and lightly over all the sharp edges to produce a fine burn and soften the edges.

6-5 Woodburning pattern for suggested design on bookends.

3. Use a thin acrylic, burnt umber wood stain for the flat back ring, a band around the face of each bookend, and the entire back.

4. Proceed with the finishing as explained in the general directions. Glue the finished flat back ring in position on the face of each bookend.

5. Attach the metal base plate to each bookend. I prefer to glue a thin felt covering over the metal to avoid any chance of it scratching another surface later.

It was my original intention to mount a raised gold monogram in the ring on each bookend, but my family talked me out of that idea. But you can suit yourself when you make your bookends.

Why Not Woodburn a Lamp Base?

Lamps are always an important part of any room's decor. And in many other crafts (such as ceramics, macrame, decorative painting, and so on) the craftsperson learns how to make or decorate lamp bases as a matter of course. If you are a woodburner, you need not feel left out because several types of unfinished wooden lamp bases are available for your use. The lamp pictured is made from a complete kit (unfinished, assembled base with electrical component parts—not the shade) that is manufactured by Corner Cupboard Crafts and is sold in many craft supply shops.

The measurements of this lamp base are 5½" x 5½" x 16½", while

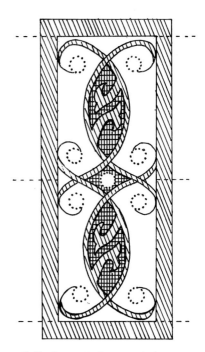

6–6 Why not woodburn a lamp to match your decor?

6–7 Suggested repeat design pattern for side panels of lamp base. Solid lines indicate line burning; squared areas, stained wood; diagonal lined areas, mottled shading.

the overall height of the lamp base with shade is approximately 30". It was simple to alternate bands of mottled shade burning and stained wood on the base and top of this lamp base as you can see. I ran into difficulties on the side panels (my own fault), and I would like to share this with you so you will avoid any similar difficulty.

After staining the vertical tooled band on each corner of the lamp base, the flat surface of the side panels remaining to be woodburned were each 3" x 14". My original plan had been to use the repeat design sketched here. Two repeats of that design fit the panel well. I quickly woodburned one panel and liked the effect, so turned the base over to continue woodburning the same design on the other sides.

I forgot one of the primary rules. Carefully consider all sides of a project to determine that the planned, repeat design will be equally effective everywhere and know what you want to burn overall before you start woodburning in any one limited area.

When I turned to that next panel on the lamp base, one-third of that panel was a very dark reddish color. It was so visible and different from the rest of the wood in the base that it either had to be emphasized or disguised within the design. The light shading and fine lines of my original design could not accomplish either. By using an enlarged version of the original design, with larger areas of stained wood incorporated, and darker shading, it was possible to disguise the large vertical strip of dark wood on that panel. The end result was that two opposite panels were decorated with the original design, while the other two have a darker

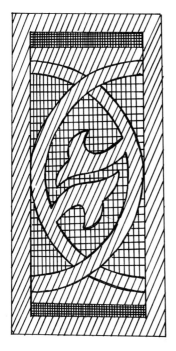

6–8 Enlarged version of same motif as in repeat design. This was used as central design unit on alternate sides of the lamp base.

6–9 Design unit to be used above and below 6–8 on darker sides of lamp to conceal variance in color of wood.

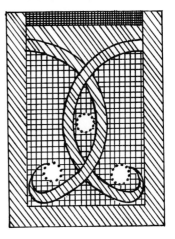

appearance and three rectangular design units on them. How much easier it would have been to examine the entire surface of the lamp base and plan the design to take care of all eventualities, rather than face them in the midst of the actual woodburning.

Repeat designs are very useful when woodburning furniture or home accessories. The use of them may make it easier for you to design something that will repeat the motifs that already dominate your decor.

Design 6–10 is appropriate to woodburn on drawer fronts, as well as

6–10 Suggested repeat design motif for drawer fronts or continuous bands.

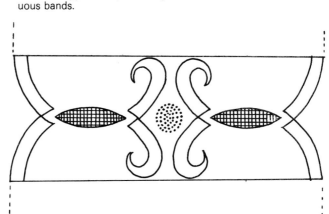

in a continuous border or band. Whether there is a center drawer pull to take the place of the dotted, central circle on the design or whether there are two drawer knobs to position on the grid areas, either can be accommodated. Plus, this design gives you an opportunity to add your individual touches.

You can mottle shade the entire background around the repeated designs. Dark flat plane shading on the curved bands in the design is for emphasis. If you need a wider design, add another band of shade or line burning on each side of the basic design. Need a longer design and do not want to repeat? Make the space between the curved bands in the center wider. These designs are usually more effective if they are repeated in a continuous fashion.

Let's say you have woodburned the design on each drawer front of a chest of drawers. Now you would like a continuous, center band down each side of that chest. Measure the space on the side that you would like covered by the woodburned design. This is a 2¼" x 6" repeat design. For example, if you want a 3¼" x 36" design band on your space, you could repeat the basic design six times for the length. Add two ¼" bands on each side to increase the width. One of these bands can be shaded to frame the basic design band. You might want to add another dotted circle in the diamond-shaped space that will appear between each double repeat of the basic design. Yes, you probably will have room to add a petal flower or star in that space, rather than the circle. However, they would not particularly suit the simple, clean lines of this design and might not give the effect you desire.

What if the length of your space to be covered is not exactly divisible by 6" (the length of the basic design)? Divide the extra length measurement by the number of full repeats you can use—plus 1. Space each repeat design that much farther apart to use up that measurement, and start and end the basic design that much farther from the beginning and end of the band. Add the burned dot circle in the center of the larger space between the repeated basic design.

If you would like to have a border around the edges of the sides and around the top of the chest, rather than a center panel, reduce the whole design in half. Then the repeat measurements will be 1⅛" x 3", better proportioned for such a border and yet retaining the features to match the larger design on the drawer front.

Perhaps you would like to apply the petal burn stroke and enjoy the ease of burning it quickly. You would probably like a repeat border, using that burn stroke. Design 6–11 is for you. It has repeat measurements of 2" x 4¼". Its outside border band reminds one of cross-stitching. Pencil mark ¼" spaces along each side of the outside band. Then simply dash burn diagonally twice, joining these dots on each side of the band, to create this effect. This repeat design can be reduced to almost any size and still will be relatively simple to woodburn.

A little more difficult and more time-consuming to woodburn, yet

6-11   Petal burns and dash burned "cross-stitching" are the main elements in this informal repeat design.

impressive, is design 6–12. It features a stylized tulip that is such a popular motif in many types of crafts. The repeat measurements are 1½" x 6¼". Certainly, you can add woodburned bands (which may be shaded, natural, and outlined, or "cross-stitched") to give width to this design if desired. But the long, narrow aspect of the original is something you want to retain.

On the drawing the diagonal lined areas indicate where mottle shade burning is used, but you can vary it by shading the grid areas shown and grid burning the diagonal lined areas. Any measurement adjustment in length should usually be made between the repeats of this basic design. You can burn a grid area between the repeats to provide continuity without detracting from the basic tulip motif.

On a long drawer front, try burning the basic design under each of the two drawer pulls. One basic design under the center drawer knob on a shorter drawer is very effective.

There are three or four samples of repeat designs sketched in this book. If you need such a design, why not sit down with a scratch pad, pencil, ruler, and compass and try designing similar ones of your own? Books and catalogs, showing inlaid wood borders, are full of possible ideas that may spur your creativity. Do not overlook simple geometric shapes. Checkerboard squares alone can be used to create an attention-compelling border as you can see on our pictured sign. It usually hangs beside our driveway, which is partially obscured and easy to miss if you do not notice the sign.

6-12   This stylized tulip repeat design can be adapted for use on many folk art projects. It is also delightful when used as the only motif in borders and bands.

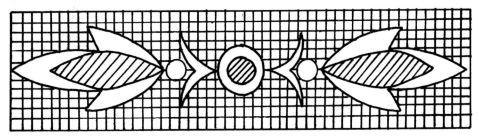

6-13 The checkered border may remind you of the Indianapolis 500, but it also draws attention to our driveway sign.

Backgammon Table

Backgammon is a popular pastime in many homes today. The triangles and spaces of a backgammon board combine to make an interesting design, even when no one is playing the game. Craftsmen have often made such boards with inlaid designs or painted triangular spaces, but few have incorporated the ease and beauty of woodburning with the making of this game board. Why not try it? (See the basic playing field in drawing 6-14.)

The measurements can be varied slightly to adapt to the size of the board on which you are burning it. For example, to enlarge the basic playing field from 16½" square, you can put ¼" spaces between the triangles and/or leave more space in the center of the board. You can border the basic playing field with bands of alternating shaded and natural strips. The triangular spaces must be large enough to accommodate the size markers with which you play. The circular ones, contained in inexpensive commercial backgammon sets, are usually 1¼" diameter.

Using a metal edge ruler as a guide, when burning, makes the basic woodburning just a matter of time if you have lightly pencil sketched an accurate outline of the playing field. After the entire outline is line burned, half the triangular spaces should be left natural while the other half are darkly mottle shaded. (Consult the drawing for the location of each.) The center space of the playing field can be painted or wood stained. Your choice will probably depend upon how attractive the figure on your particular piece of wood is.

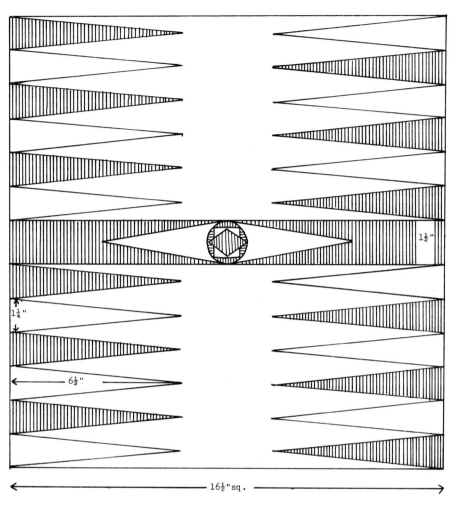

6–14 Measurement drawing of backgammon playing field.

At Christmas we woodburned several backgammon games for gifts, using a high grade of plywood (bordered with quarter round) as the board. But our daughter bought this small unfinished end table and requested that her game be woodburned on it. The playing field took up the entire top of this little table so you might want to choose a larger table on which the game board would be a center top design only. Just be sure the players can conveniently reach over the playing field. If your family members are avid checker players, could you woodburn a checkerboard instead? Of course—even more easily than the backgammon one.

Since the drawers in this backgammon table will undoubtedly be used to store the playing pieces and dice, a geometric design was also used on the drawer fronts to suggest that. A more modern drawer front motif would have been to just have an elongated triangle reaching from each drawer side to the pull in the center, eliminating the circles and swirls.

6–15 Topped by a woodburned playing field, this table is always ready for a quick game of backgammon.

6–16 Drawer fronts of table also are decorated with woodburned designs.

The figure on this unfinished table was obvious and attractive, yet the wood was too light colored to match the rest of my daughter's furniture. Look at the picture and you will see the original color evidenced by the natural portions on the playing field. Fruitwood, acrylic wood stain, thinned and brushed and wiped overall (except for the woodburned portions of the playing field) darkened the table to the desired degree. A few extra coats of wood finish overall provided the fine depth of finish that is characteristic of fine furniture.

Because these coats were hand rubbed with a fine finishing pad between every two coats of finish, the glossy surface feels just as smooth as it looks. Enough coats of finish can be applied to even submerge the feel of the woodburned lines and the texture of the shaded areas, though that is not necessary. Now, when people see this backgammon table, they say "How did you do that? Is it inlaid or a veneer?" So far, no one has guessed that it is a woodburned design.

Clothes Hook Plaque

My sweater hanger in my office is decorative, yet very practical. No attempt was made to hide the hook (even though we failed to screw it in place on the medallion before the picture was taken). The center medallion draws attention to it so that people will not be fooled by the decorative floral border and will surely know its intended use.

6-17 It is actually a clothes hook plaque, though we forgot to screw the ceramic hook into place on the medallion before the picture was taken.

Adco Redwood Co. makes these 6" x 9" oval redwood plaques with a pretooled and stained edge, which are available in most craft supply shops. You can use any oval plaque of similar size and then shade burn the sides or stain them yourself if you can not find them locally.

Note that just a basic outline is given in the pattern 6–18. Please look closely at the pictured plaque. The shading of half the leaves, on the medallion, the separation of the petals of the flower, and the dash strokes bordering the petals and around the dotted center are left to your freehand burning, after the basic outline has been line burned. The procedure for finishing is just as in the general directions in chapter 2.

6-18 Notice you are just given the basic outline here. Study the picture and line, dot, shade burn, and so on inside the outline to give added detail and interest.

Maybe Sister would hang up her pajamas in the morning when she dresses if she had a decorative clothes hook plaque in her room. And if she doesn't, it still looks good on the wall! Speaking of projects for children's rooms, wait until you meet this character.

Grandma Duck

Mother Goose is not a stranger to most children so it is to be expected that they will quickly relate to her cousin, Grandma Duck. When I received the unfinished wood, cutout duck plaque from Corner Cupboard Crafts, Inc., there was a pattern and instructions with it on how to paint a folk art design on it. Actually, had I not been so intent on creating a Grandma Duck design to use on accessories for a tiny child's room or bathroom, it would have been simple to just woodburn that folk art design on the plaque and have a conventional wall decoration.

These sketches will show you how these ducks might be used. A

6-19 Introducing Grandma Duck, cousin to Mother Goose.

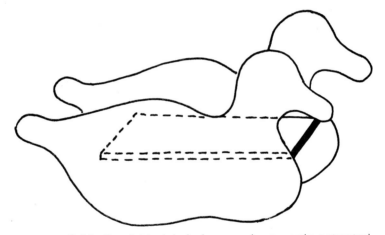

6-20 Two finished duck plaques and a step make a stepstool.

wooden step (glued and secured with screws) between two finished ducks will make a charming small child's stepstool. Or two hangers, attached to the back of the Grandma Duck plaque, in positions indicated by X on the sketches, will enable you to hang her on the wall. The addition of a towel bar or clothes hooks will make her into a useful towel or clothes rack.

The same basic design can be woodburned on the front or top of an unfinished toy chest. If the decorating mother is a home sewer, you might expect to see a continued use of the Grandma Duck motif—appliquéd or quilted on a bed coverlet and curtains.

But back to the work of woodburning the Grandma Duck image on the unfinished cutout plaque.

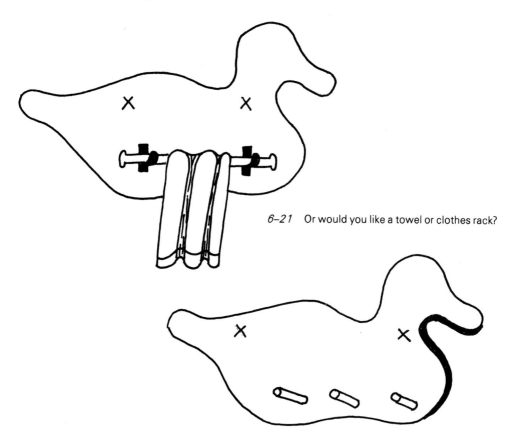

6–21 Or would you like a towel or clothes rack?

1. As always, preparing the plaque and then applying the design is first. On a cutout plaque such as this, plan to do a little additional sanding on the edges and around the sharper edges slightly so there will be no possibility of splinters later.

You can enlarge the pattern in drawing 6–22 by using the grid method, and then trace it on the plaque. Actually, by using the curves and shape of the duck plaque as reference points, it is relatively simple to pencil-sketch Grandma Duck and her bib and tucker right on the plaque, without having to do any tracing or enlarging.

2. Most of the woodburning on this design is line burning. Notice drawing 6–23, which is the feather detail. Dark flat plane shading between and around the tips of the feathers accent them and give them more dimension. The same shading is used on limited areas of the bill. Closely spaced, burned dots in the border around the jacket and its sleeve develop a rough texture appearance, while the design on the bib is burned with the petal stroke. Carry the design over the edges of the plaque so that Grandma Duck will be attractive and complete from any angle. (You can woodburn the same design on the inside of the two ducks if you are making the footstool, or simply finish the inside natural or paint it to match the step.)

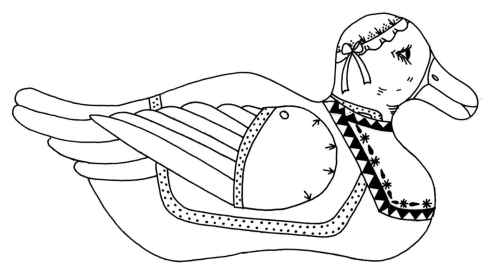

6-22   Basic pattern for woodburning Grandma Duck.

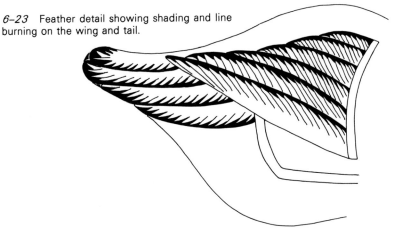

6-23   Feather detail showing shading and line burning on the wing and tail.

Did you observe that the lapping waves along Grandma Duck's bottom in the picture are missing from the pattern? This was deliberate because if I were burning her again I would omit the waves. You are told this now to remind you how important it is to know exactly what you want in the design before you start burning. Once you have woodburned an element into a design, it is permanent and cannot be erased.

3. After the woodburning is completed and the duck plaque is rubbed overall with a fine finishing pad, cherry and fruitwood acrylic wood stain is used to color the jacket, bib, and cap. They contrast effectively with the natural color of the pine and yet allow the figure of the wood to show. This gives the appearance, almost, of shimmering fabric after the final finish is applied. Touches of green acrylic paint on the ribbon on the cap, the button on the jacket, and on half the triangles around the

bib's border provide just a slight color accent, highlighting the other varied wood tones. Any other bright complimentary color would be as effective.

4. Finishing properly, as described in general procedures in chapter 2, is very important in this project, as is using a wood finish that is water resistant and nontoxic. Obviously, if Grandma Duck is to be used in a child's room, she will have to be washed often. With the proper finish, she will last indefinitely and possibly become one of your family's favorite hand-me-downs.

Floral Footstool with Lady Bugs

6–24   Top view of floral footstool with resident lady bugs.

The shape of this footstool so intrigued me that I never noticed the two large knots on the top surface when I purchased it in a craft supply shop. But when it came time to plan a design to be woodburned on it, those knots were hard to conceal and hard to burn. I felt the design had to incorporate the curved lines of the stool's top but still should be subtle enough to avoid too much busyness. Big problem? No, not really. The knots seemed to resemble friendly little garden bugs so a floral design could be used. Developing the suggestion of flowers with clean geomet-

6–25   Side view of woodburned footstool.

ric figures (just using shaded and unshaded areas and no heavily burned lines), fitted into the outside dimensions of the stool, solved this problem, at least to my satisfaction.

Here is what you do if you wish to duplicate this design on a footstool of your own. You will need your compass in this project. Need I remind you that you should thoroughly sand the footstool before applying the design? You have that rule firmly in mind by now, don't you?

1. Use a ruler and pencil to measure and sketch a light line all around the top, ¼" in from the outside edge.

2. Find the exact center of each half of the footstool top. Use a compass to lightly draw a 5¾" diameter circle on each half. Still using the compass, draw intersecting half circles on that 5¾" diameter circle until you have twelve large outside flower petals and twelve small inner petals (see drawing 6–26).

6–26 Basic pattern for woodburning top of footstool.

3. Between these two large circles (in the middle of the footstool), draw a 2¼" diameter circle. It should just barely touch each outer circle if you have measured accurately. Inside that 2¼" circle, draw a 2" circle and intersect it until you have six petals.

4. Use the compass and the drawing to determine the placement of the other band lines around the floral centers.

5. Shade burn the areas indicated by the lined portions on the drawing. It illustrates just enough of the whole to guide you in burning the whole design. Note the areas where dots are burned for accents.

6. On the legs, a shade burned ¼" band (placed ¼" in from the outside edges of the legs) provides just a touch of interest there. Too much detail would detract from the top design.

7. If you have "lady bug" knots on your footstool, you can add legs and so on with the pyrolectric pen. Be sure to erase all your pencil marks after the woodburning is completed and before you proceed with the usual steps of finishing.

"Dubl Handi" Washboard

6–27 Useful and decorative, a "Dubl Handi" washboard becomes a woodburned bulletin board.

When you travel in a mini motor home, you will find many of the items you carry along will have to do double duty. This small washboard lived up to its name, "Dubl Handi," coined by the manufacturer. Though George said that he doubted that very many campers toted a woodburned, decorated washboard along with them!

Actually, hanging on the closet door between washings, the washboard also serves as a bulletin board, an informal serving tray, or a makeshift cutting board. Little magnets are used on the center metal section to hold slips of message paper. It really was not our intention to disguise what the washboard was, rather to make it look old and more attractive.

It did not take long to flat plane shade the outer areas of the legs and then use rod and petal burn strokes to create an old-fashioned border design. Drawing 6–28 illustrates how to burn this border. I used the stylized tulip design (6–12) on the top of the washboard, but you cannot

6–28 Woodburning detail for sides of washboard.

see it in the photograph. The rest, finishing and so on, is the same basic procedure as always.

Think about decorating one of these small unfinished washboards (which you can purchase in most hardware stores) for a young college girl to use as a bulletin board. The sanding and finishing you do with the woodburning makes it smoother and less apt to snag fragile materials when it is used as a washboard. It can even be packed into a suitcase safely, as the manufacturer suggests. Personally, I like the conversations it inspires.

Christmas Bells

6–29 Woodburned in 1977, this holiday bell still delivers its message every Christmas.

These are only visible during the holiday season as home accessories, but let's share a family joke that accidentally has become a Christmas tradition at our house. Back in the early months of 1976, the centennial year, I purchased a number of large unfinished wooden replicas of the Liberty Bell from Corner Cupboard Crafts, Inc. These bells were intended for use in a rather ambitious patriotic project.

Now, maybe you have never started a craft project and then procrastinated on finishing it until the occasion was long past for which it was intended. That is one of my worst faults, and it gives rise to a lot of teasing from my whole family. So I just had to do something with those bells. Obviously, since you see the picture, my solution was to woodburn and finish in 1977 a Christmas bell with the greeting "Merry Christmas" that could hang on our mailbox during the season. The next year, another message, "Peace On Earth" on a woodburned bell, hung by our nameplate beside the driveway. The one for the garage door, "Happy New Year," still is not finished, but my older children look every year for the message bells, when they come home for the holidays.

If you want to woodburn some similar Christmas bells and cannot find

6–30 Shading around letters, rather than outlining them with heavier burned lines, gives a much softer appearance.

6–31 Measurements of the Christmas bell.

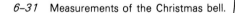

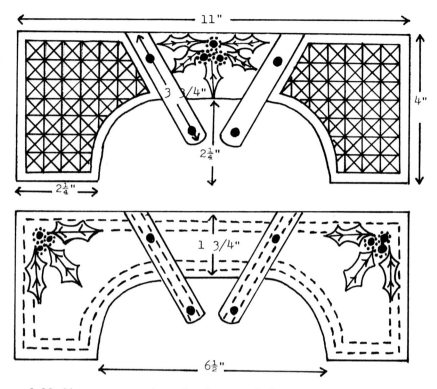

6–32 Measurements and woodburning steps for hanger on Christmas bells.

6–33 Suggested pattern for woodburning Christmas bell.

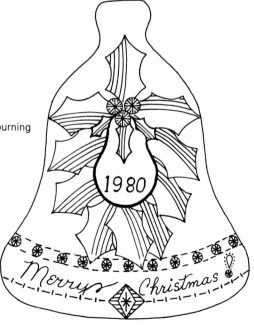

unfinished ones in your craft supply store—since the centennial fever has subsided—the measurements of the bell and hanger are given here. You can cut them (or have them cut) from ½" to ¾" thick pine.

You will not want to trace these designs that I used because you will have no trouble drawing most of the details right on the wooden bell's surface, using a ruler and pencil. Besides, you certainly want to incorporate your own ideas. Let me give you a few hints.

If you have difficulty line burning small letters, use a burned dotted line instead. Or mottle shade burn the areas around the letters (indicated by vertical lines around "Peace On Earth" on the drawing) and leave the letters natural. Pine burns very quickly and may make it difficult for a beginner to achieve very fine lines. Use dashes to burn a broken line then. It appears to be lighter than just one heavily burned continuous line. Two rows of dashes, with shading between them, resembles saddle-stitching as you can see on the border around the one bell's hanger.

6–34 Or another suggestion for woodburning a message.

Dairymaid Stool

Are you still afraid to strike out burning freehand? Why not try something very simple like the folk art type designs on this little stool? Use your compass and lightly pencil mark some reference points to keep your design well spaced. Think about the shapes of the basic burn strokes, their combinations, and so on, and plan a design on paper using

6-35 Purposely half finished, this dairymaid stool top illustrates how finish can change the appearance of a woodburned project.

them. In our case we drew an 8½" diameter circle around a 7" diameter circle, then a 5½" diameter circle around a heart. Arrows, dots, zigzags, simple flowers with leaves, and so on were then evenly spaced and burned on those circles. Different four- and eight-cluster petal burns were spaced evenly around the edge of the stool.

6-36 This stool was decorated with the very simplest, freehand burn strokes. This is a good beginning point for the timid woodburner who still insists on burning only on traced designs.

It is possible that you might want a design that resembles more closely the usual folk art motifs. Make a solid floral band between the 8½" and 5½" circles. Or maybe you would like to use the suggested design 6-37. Sketch your design lightly on the band and then burn. Do not forget to use the large eraser to rub away any excess pencil marks before you proceed with the finishing.

So, you noticed in the picture that we had only completed one half

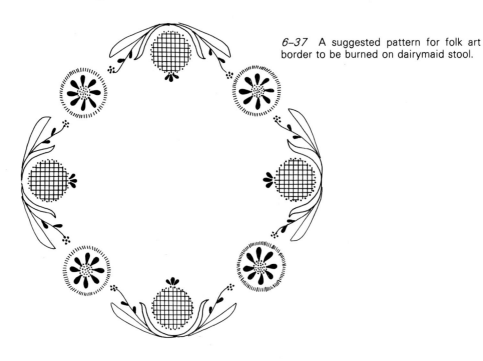

6-37 A suggested pattern for folk art border to be burned on dairymaid stool.

of the finishing of this dairymaid stool. Right, we were hoping a visual reminder of how much better finished woodburned wood looks and wears would make a point with you. If it does, you will resolve right now not to skip the finishing touches on your work after the woodburning is completed.

Photo Plaques

When is a picture frame not a frame? When it is really a flat redwood plaque that has had a border woodburned in a rectangular area to make a designed enclosure for a 5" x 7" photograph, which is glued in position. What protects the picture from soil and fingerprints as it hangs on the wall? An overlay sheet of glass. It was cut to size, and corner holes were drilled at the glass company from which it was purchased. It is held in place by four decorative corner screws, which are also available at the glass company or at the local hardware store.

Do you ever make mistakes when finishing a craft project? Do you like to know what pitfalls you might encounter? If your answer is "yes," you will understand why I decided to leave the serious mistake I made on one of these picture plaques visible in the photograph, rather than correct it. If you tighten the decorative screws too tightly or use screws that are too large for the drilled holes, when attaching the glass to the plaque, it is possible to shatter the glass around the drilled hole. With four screws holding the glass in position, it is not necessary to forcibly tighten them as I did. Just screw them in snugly and do not try to see how tight

6–38 Photograph plaques provide a unique way to frame your favorite photographs.

you can get them. Now you are forewarned that if you crack the glass in this fashion, it must be replaced.

Why aren't the borders on these three pictures all alike? Because I wanted to show you three very simple designs and hope that they will inspire you to make up your own.

But let's backtrack and talk about the woodburned borders on these picture plaques. The dark band was already on the Adco redwood plaques that I used, so the woodburned design was concentrated within it. You can easily burn the same ½" wide band on your plaque if it is not there and if you would like it.

Usually there is a white band around the edges of a color photograph that needs to be trimmed off before you mount the picture. Besides you need to know what the exact outside measurements of your specific photograph are. Center space a rectangle of that correct size on the plaque and pencil sketch the outline so you can adjust your design to fit it.

As you can see, design 6–39 is the easiest and fastest to accomplish. To copy it yourself, burn a ¼" wide "saddle-stitch" band ¼" within the outside dark strip. Then burn another such band around your center photo space. (Remember, a saddle-stitch band is just two rows of burned dashes, ¼" apart, with mottled shade burning between the dashes.)

To add color to this border, you can choose one of the colors from the picture and paint a 1" wide acrylic strip of that color between the saddle-stitch bands. Actually, rather than painting it, you can burn a casual floral design or Western motif in that strip. How appropriate such a plaque would be then to encircle the picture of some individual in Western attire or maybe your favorite horse photograph.

The ripple look of the border on one of the picture plaques is detailed in figure 6–40. It shows you the steps.

6–39 Bands of "saddle stitching" on each side of a painted color band border the photograph space.

6–40 Steps to sketch and burn the "ripple" look border on a plaque.

6-41 Sketching and woodburning guide for rickrack border for photograph plaque.

1. Lightly pencil draw a gridwork of ¼" squares in a 1¾" wide strip within the rectangular dark band.

2. Line burn only the vertical lines of the squares.

3. Pencil sketch a wavy line along each of the horizontal lines of the squares, going below the line in one square and above the line in the next, and so on (see drawing).

4. Line burn the wavy, horizontal lines.

5. Mottle shade burn alternate squares. (You are right. They really are not technically squares anymore since two of the lines of each are curved.) By the way, this ripple design can be used very effectively on a small rectangular tabletop.

For that matter, so would design 6–41. You hardly need any instructions to follow when burning this design. Once you have pencil drawn a series of 1" base x ½" high triangles within the dark rectangular band and around the center photograph space, you will line burn them. Then all that is left to burn is the mottle shading in the triangles.

Before you start drawing your triangles with your pencil and ruler, notice on the drawing how the corners are designed. If you start measuring from a center point on each side and work out from that point, you can adjust the corner measurements slightly to disguise small discrepancies in your measurements. We all endeavor to measure very accurately, but sometimes the width of the pencil marks can cause slight variations, or the existing dark rectangular band might not have been tooled to fine accuracy.

Who are the children in the pictures? My grandchildren, of course. In our family everyone is into crafts in one form or another.

7 THE USE OF THE PYROLECTRIC PEN ON OTHER MATERIALS

In a book devoted to woodburning, it would probably be a mistake to emphasize too much that the same pyrolectric pen can be used effectively on other materials. These could include cloth, leather, and paper, as well as wood substitutes such as particle or composition board and air drying modeling wood. In fact, if you concentrated on this aspect of burning with the pyrolectric pen, you could craft enough projects to fill another book. But that is not my intention so just enough projects have been included here to visually remind you of these possible uses of your woodburning tool.

Burning on Cloth

Because there are so many kinds of fabrics, both man-made and natural, it is not safe to generalize that you can burn designs equally as well on any and all cloth. Many synthetics, such as nylon, melt so quickly, when touched with the hot pen point, that it is difficult to work fast enough to avoid making a "melted" hole in the fabric. It is safe to advise you to test a scrap of the cloth that you intend to burn before you progress too far into planning your project. Pin or tack your piece of cloth smoothly and tautly over an aluminum foil covered composition board (like a ceiling tile or macramé board).

I have never had a piece of cloth actually burst into flame because naturally, if it shows signs of melting from the heat of the pen point, I

130

7–1 A cloth laundry bag gains a certain degree of individualism because of its burned design combined with yarn flowers.

remove the point from the cloth. The heat of the pen point is not the same as using a match near the cloth, and you are actually lightly "scorching" a design on the cloth, not burning it in the sense of creating flame with a match.

In this burning test you will seek to discover:

1. How hot a pen point is required to burn this particular cloth? On the laundry bag pictured, the fabric was a heavy wash and wear material that had been treated to retain its wrinkled appearance. As is often the case today, the cloth was a blend of natural cotton and man-made fibers. A 100-watt bulb was used in the plug series tap of the pyrolectric pen. Though use of a 75-watt bulb is usually recommended when burning cloth, in this case it burned too slowly. On a lighter or thinner fabric, with more man-made fiber content, the 100-watt heat might have burned too quickly for convenient control. So you need to test and experiment until the temperature of your pen is satisfactory for your cloth.

2. How does the texture of this material affect the burning process? If you have the cloth stretched tautly so it does not drag along with the pen point as you burn, you can minimize the influence of the texture. Naturally, a smooth texture tends to be easier to burn since it does not deflect, or catch, the pen point as you burn. If you wish to burn a coarsely woven, rough-textured cloth, practice on your scraps so you learn to control the pen firmly. Keep your woodburning pen point clean so the excess carbon does not smudge the cloth.

3. Can the basic burn strokes be used on cloth? It is much easier to burn clear down through the cloth than it is on wood. Therefore, you strive to learn to burn quickly, using moderate pressure on the pen, and avoid letting the pen point burn in one spot too long.

Line, shading, and dash burn strokes are relatively easy to burn on cloth, as are quickly burned small dots. But do not expect to be able to hold the pen point tip on the cloth and rotate it for larger dots as you can do on wood. Petal, rod, and V-edge burn strokes are seldom used on cloth.

You will find the subtle, warm brown appearance of a design burned on cloth is very effective and well worth the preproject testing you have done.

I am often asked "How well do burned designs on cloth launder? How long do the designs last before they fade?" They launder well, but I have never really tested how long they last without fading. How long do your other laundered fabrics last before they fade? It depends upon your washing methods and the fabric. In my unscientific experience, long exposure to bright sunlight is more apt to fade the burned design than washing. Those of you who have ever scorched linens or clothing when ironing know those burns last a long time.

7–2   Designed and burned by Regina Petrutis, this woodland scene illustrates the use of a pyrolectric pen on soft composition board.
Picture courtesy Regina Petrutis

Burning on Composition Board

Regina Petrutis, an artist that you will read more about in chapter 8, loaned us a picture of a design burned on composition board. Since this material is very porous and burns rapidly, the lines and shading on it are apt to be quite dark and relatively heavy. Plus there is no obvious figure or grain apparent on the composition board and little, if any, color. Therefore, these designs normally are planned to cover as much of the surface as possible.

In Regina's mushroom design, note how the continuous lines burned in the background emphasize the lighter color of the mushrooms and foliage. The dark and light burned border lines encompass and frame the scene. When she mounted this scene on a strongly patterned wood, she added to the importance of the burned design, increased the feeling of a woodland scene, and provided protection for the soft edges of the center composition board panel.

Burning on Leather

In youth group activities and at some adult functions, name tags play an important role in getting acquainted. When George and I taught at the Hoosier Recreation Workshop, each participant was given a blank leather medallion and told to make a name tag out of it. Tradition had it that anyone would be penalized (gently) if they appeared anytime, anywhere, throughout the week of the workshop without the name tag. Since I was demonstrating and teaching about woodburning and clay craft, naturally my name tag was handmade to emphasize those crafts.

7–3 a. b. c. There is no question about who owns each name tag, but which two are leather? The Jo tag is actually air drying modeling wood.

Truthfully, I had never burned on leather before that time, but knew it would work because I had seen cattle branded.

Which all leads to our discussion of how to burn on leather. (I have done a lot more burning on leather since then, but still prefer to burn on wood.) Leather burns under the pyrolectric pen like softwood without grain or pattern. If you have a light touch and work very quickly, you may be able to use a 100-watt bulb in the pyrolectric pen's plug series tap. But a pen equipped with a 75-watt bulb in the series tap should burn more satisfactorily, thus providing a lower temperature. When using other type woodburning pens than the pyrolectric with the series tap, these pens will usually have overpoints designed for use on leather. Using such a tip will cut down the heat of that pen point.

The easiest leather upon which to burn is light colored, reasonably soft, and undyed. Cover a ceiling tile or similar size board with aluminum foil. Stretch the portion of leather upon which you are going to burn over this board. Pin or tack it so you have a taut area where the design will be.

Sketch or trace your pattern on the leather. Do not press too hard so you make indentations in the leather. Choose a relatively simple design for your first attempt. Test the temperature of the pen point and practice your strokes on a scrap piece of this same leather to familiarize yourself with how this particular leather burns. Each type of leather has its own characteristics.

When burning on leather, it is especially important to remember that the amount of pressure needed on the pen is not great. Do not use too much pressure. The leather burns very quickly, and you need only leave the pen point in position on it lightly and very briefly to burn a deep brown stroke. Burn your lines lightly at first and then go back over them if you want them darker, deeper, or wider. There is no grain or pattern to deflect the pen point, but if you attempt to burn deep, wide continuous lines all at once, the pen point has a tendency to drag and sink deeper than desired into the soft leather. Most shading on leather will be quite dark because the leather burns so quickly. You will find it easy to write script or create curved designs on the leather with just the tip of the pen point.

Keep your pen point clean while burning. Excess carbon particles can smudge the leather. You cannot sand the burned design on the leather as you would on wood, but you can wipe off the design with a soft cloth to remove the excess carbon.

Burning on Modeling Wood

Once you are addicted to working with the pyrolectric pen, you will always be alert to finding new materials upon which to burn. General Crafts Corporation sent me a sample of their air drying modeling wood. Their claims of "easy to use, nontoxic, no shrinkage, hardens without kiln firing, takes on all the properties of real wood, etc." spurred me on to experimenting.

Boreado modeling wood resembles clay when you start modeling it. It can be shaped just like clay by rolling it into a slab and cutting it with a round doughnut cutter (without the center hole) to make a name tag or kerchief slide like those pictured. Or you can "pat" mold it over half a Styrofoam egg to make a dried flower pocket as we did.

After drying at least twenty-four hours, it does take on some of the properties of wood, but has no pattern or grain. You can cut it with a serrated knife, sand it, draw on it with a pencil; it is light tan and darkens slightly when finish is applied. But the surprise comes when you begin to woodburn this pseudo-wood. Thinking of its composition and original form, I first tried using a 60-watt bulb in the pyrolectric pen's plug series tap—no burning effect on this artificial wood! A hot pen point (100-watt bulb in series tap) burned into it very slowly as though you were burning a very hard wood.

Any of the basic burn strokes can be used on this dry modeling wood. Its slow-burning characteristic makes it possible to burn very fine lines and petal burns on it. It certainly would lend itself well to intricate designs, but it takes longer to burn on it.

7-4 Air drying modeling wood can be used to add another dimension to a plaque. It can be woodburned as though it really were a hard wood.

Burning on Particle Board

Since burning on particle board is quite similar to burning on a medium hard wood, it seemed you might enjoy a genuine how-to project here. You might think that a tool carryall like this one would surely require the services of a carpenter. It does make a faster task of finishing

7–5   A carryall for tools, made of particle board, is distinctively decorated with woodburning and accents of bright acrylic color.

this project if you can buy a ready-made unfinished tool carryall of wood or particle board. Actually, I am about the furthest thing from a capable carpenter, but with the aid of some strong furniture glue, a large staple gun, and precut pieces, the carryall pictured was constructed by me. George cut out all the pieces from a sheet of ⅜" thick particle board that can be purchased from a lumberyard or a family center type hardware store. The handle is oak for strength.

To make the carryall:

1. Cut two rectangular side pieces each 4¼" x 14¼" x ⅜". Cut one rectangular bottom base 13¾" x 6" x ⅜". Cut two end pieces (see drawing 7–6 for the shape) each 6" x 7½" x ⅜". The oak handle measures 1¼" x 13¾" x ¾".

2. Fit the pieces together to be sure they are aligned properly before you start gluing or stapling them together. The end pieces should come down and cover the bottom edge of the base (see drawing 7–7). The sides cover the bottom edges of the base and the side edges of the ends. The handle fits between the ends at their narrow top.

When you are certain that each piece fits properly, glue and staple the pieces together. Do not get slap happy when you are using the staple gun. On drawing 7–7, notice the dashes that indicate where staples should be placed. Also, apply the glue sparingly and only on the edges of the pieces because surplus glue, if it dribbles onto the flat surfaces, many cause difficulties later when you are finishing the design areas. Wait until the glue is thoroughly dry before handling the tool carryall.

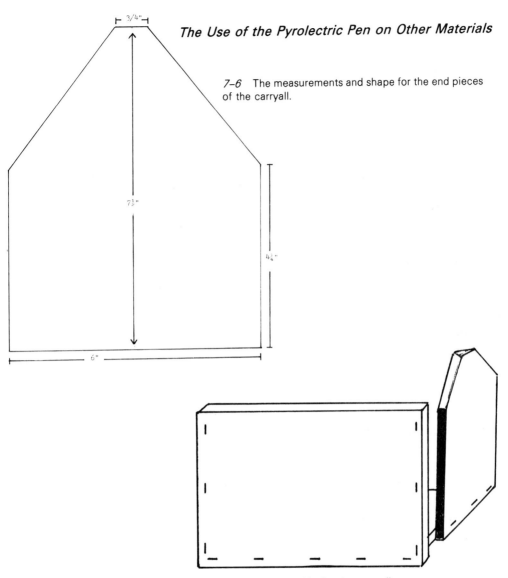

7–6   The measurements and shape for the end pieces of the carryall.

7–7   An assembly guide for the carryall.

Here are the steps to follow in applying your design to the carryall.

3. Center and pencil sketch the lettered panel (drawing 7–8) on the front of the carryall. *Do not burn it or paint it yet!* Drawing 7–9 is half of a suggested floral design that you can sketch over the lettered panel. Match the spot marked X on the drawing with a point on the bottom edge of the front that is 7¼" from the left end. Sketch the pattern along the bottom and up over the left end of the lettered panel. Glance at the photograph to see how the stem and leaves cover parts of the lettering.

Next reverse the design and sketch it along the top and down over the right end of the lettered panel.

Do not forget to decorate the back too. It will look fine with just a similar floral design, or you can add a personalized touch by adding the owner's name here.

7–8 Suggested lettering guide for the front of the carryall.

7–9 Use this floral design or one of your own to twine over lettering panel on the front of the carryall.

4. Sketch the pattern in drawing 7–11 on each end of the carryall. Now you are ready to woodburn the design.

5. Line burn the outlines of the entire design. Shade burn the letters and the areas of the design that are shown dotted on the drawings. When you shade burn on particle board, it looks like dark cork.

Rod burn evenly spaced grooves around all outside edges including the handle. Look at the picture for more guidance if necessary.

Rub down the woodburned areas with a fine sanding pad before applying color accents with acrylic paints. You can apply any color combination you like, and these are only suggestions. Apply orange acrylic paint to the areas indicated by lined portions on the drawings, light green to the leaves, blue to the background behind the shaded letters, and yellow centers on the flowers. Be sure the acrylic paint is thoroughly dry before you apply the usual coats of wood finish overall. The particle board darkens slightly under the finish and is much smoother and easier to clean.

While I was working on this carryall, many variations and uses came to mind. Instead of tools, how about using it to carry small potted plants to the garden? Vice versa, you could carry flowers in it to the house or let your seedlings grow in peat pots within it while it sits on a windowsill. It could also be made into a sewing box, although then you would probably want to add a lid to each side (see drawing 7–12). You would need to cut out a half circle in the middle of the lid so your hand could reach through it to grasp the handle.

If you added a lid with a catch, you could construct a smaller version for a casual purse. Little children could use a carryall for a doll and its clothes or for building blocks, and so on. Keep thinking and you will end up making several carryalls as I intend to do.

7–10 The back of the carryall is also decorated so it will be attractive from any angle.

7–11 Do not forget to woodburn a floral design on the ends.

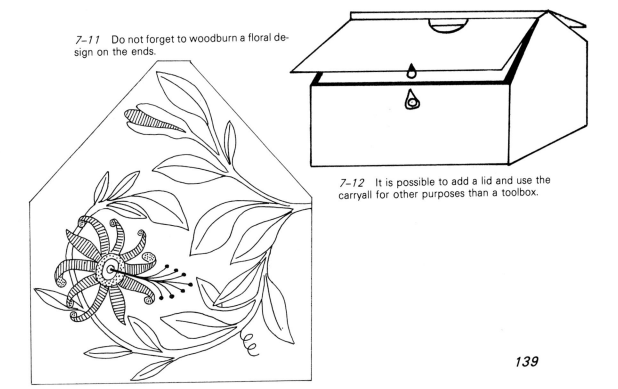

7–12 It is possible to add a lid and use the carryall for other purposes than a toolbox.

8 MEET SOME ARTISTS WHO WOODBURN

Every page, every project, and every picture in this book was expressly included to encourage you to learn to woodburn and then to see just how skillful you can become with that creative medium. The three artists you will meet in this chapter were chosen because each has developed their woodburning skill to a point where it is important in their artistic career, yet each is different. One uses woodburning to interpret European folk art designs. For another, woodburning is an accompaniment to his primary skill, wood carving. The third has developed woodburning to a fine art.

It is a recognized fact that most artists hate to have their works copied, but few will object if you study their designs and craftsmanship in order to improve your own.

Regina Petrutis, Woodburning Folk Artist

In a book that is trying to detail the progression of a technique through the craft stage to an art, it is particularly appropriate to include information about Regina Petrutis of District Heights, Maryland. Her woodburning artistry has received public recognition and commercial acceptance in the last few years, but it was not always that way. A high point of that recognition, in her own mind, was an occasion in 1978 when she received a request to create a woodburned box (featuring folk designs) for the First Lady of the United States, Mrs. Carter. During a Lithuanian

8-1 Regina Petrutis has exhibited and lectured on woodburning in many parts of the United States.
Picture courtesy Regina Petrutis

8-2 Candlesticks and music boxes by Regina Petrutis. Do the candlesticks inspire you to look around the lumberyard or building center to find potential objects for woodburning? The candle cups are available in craft supply shops, as are the unfinished boxes.
Picture courtesy Regina Petrutis

reception in the White House in November of that year, Regina presented the intricately patterned box to Mrs. Carter. In her mementos, Regina keeps clippings of the publicity and the personal thank-you letter from the First Lady that testify to the effectiveness of that gift.

Meet Some Artists Who Woodburn

In her own words, Regina shares with us the path by which she became a woodburning artist.

"I was introduced to the craft of woodburning more than twenty-five years ago while making items for a Girl Scouts' bazaar. Our craft leader showed me how to use the woodburning pen to decorate wooden items.

"My pursuit of this technique was put aside while I attended college, married, and began raising three daughters. But when my girls reached the age of Girl Scouting, I found myself involved again. This time I not only taught the girls the craft of woodburning, but also began doing a lot of it for my own enjoyment.

"I should mention that I was born in Lithuania, and this craft is very familiar to Lithuanian people as it had its origin in Eastern Europe. When I initially began spending more time woodburning, most of my work was decorating wooden items with my country's designs. After a few years of woodburning specific items for requests, displaying and selling my pieces at bazaars and local craft shows, when a local shop asked to distribute my woodburning pieces, I decided to go into business and produce items for commercial sale.

"These activities have also led to many requests to display my work and lecture at shows in many different cities—usually in Lithuanian communities—from as far away as Los Angeles. The only problem with this is that woodburning is not something that can be mass produced, and it is a slow and exact process. Though I enjoy working on the woodburned pieces, it is seldom that I can make things fast enough to satisfy the demand.

"My designs are mostly traditional folk designs that I have adapted to woodburning and to the wooden object upon which they are used. I am

8-4 Another folk art plate by Regina Petrutis. It takes accurate measurement, fine craftsmanship, as well as practice skill to create a woodburned, circular wooden tray such as this.
Picture courtesy Regina Petrutis

8-3 Bird of happiness plate by Regina Petrutis.
Picture courtesy Regina Petrutis

presently learning more about woodworking so I can design and build my own unfinished wooden jewelry boxes, and so on."

In other pictures that appeared earlier in this book, you will discover that Regina also uses some painting in combination with her woodburning in certain designs.

Phillip E. Zeller, Woodcarver

Even if you have never met Phillip Zeller, you gain an impression of the man from his decorative bird carvings. As the Bangor *Daily News* said in October 1978, "His work reveals a blend of workmanship and a keen awareness of nature. The vivid impressions presented by his carvings reflect a lifelong fascination with the out-of-doors, coupled with hours of research and first-hand observation of his subjects."

The brochure of the Owens Gallery in Oklahoma City (which represents Zeller's work) stresses how this artist must not only capture the form and flowing lines of avian beauty with knife and chisel, but also the subtleties of color and shading. In his own words, Phillip Zeller tells us how he uses woodburning in that capture of subtle shading.

"After outlining a pattern on basswood and cutting out the rough shape with a band saw, I use knives and chisels to shape the bird and carve each individual feather. Each feather is drawn in by pencil and then carved to stand out slightly from the body. In some cases, the feathers are individually carved and attached later to the body. Then I sand the piece lightly to smooth. I use the Post pyrolectric pen with an 85-watt bulb in the plug series tap to burn them. On some very thin feathers, I may cut down that wattage to avoid burning too deeply.

8–5 Ring-necked pheasant by Phillip Zeller.
Picture courtesy Phillip Zeller

"On large feathers, such as tail, wing primaries, and so on, I burn in the center shaft first and then sand the sides slightly. The side veining is then burnt in. On small feathers, the center shaft is sometimes left out and only veining is burnt.

"After the entire piece is burned, I wire brush and clean it. When it is painted in oil paints, I try as nearly as I can to resemble the coloring of the actual bird."

Zeller's work is a very good example of how woodburning can be used to advantage in conjunction with other art techniques. The fine details of his woodburned feathers and bark certainly add to his carving, but in such a subtle way that they never detract from the overall effect of his bird sculptures.

8-6 Feigning Killdeer by Phillip Zeller
Picture courtesy Phillip Zeller

8-7 Purple Gallinule by Phillip Zeller
Picture courtesy Phillip Zeller

144

Audronē Bartys, Artist

Though I have never met Audronē Bartys of New Brunswick, New Jersey, personally, I was introduced to her woodburning artistry several years ago. At that time a wood product manufacturer in New York City (Woodring Craft) had commissioned Ms. Bartys to woodburn on some of their products. When finished, her beautiful plaques and bracelets were shown in many parts of the United States where that company exhibited in hobby and craft trade shows. They received a great deal of attention and acclaim. Through the cooperation of Woodring Craft, we are able to include pictures of a few of Audronē's woodburnings so you too can admire her talent and artistry.

Her skill in burning fine, delicate lines and tiny, intricate designs and her superb workmanship, coupled with her artistic talent, give Audronē's woodburnings certain characteristics that make them easy to identify. When you look at the two character studies pictured here and at the owl in chapter 5, see how she uses light strokes of the pyrolectric pen as another artist might use an ink pen to sketch. It is obvious that she carefully considers the figure of the wood and capitalizes on its natural beauty.

Audronē's bracelets speak for themselves, telling you what some of you might aspire to accomplish for yourself someday when you become an experienced and skilled woodburner.

Will all the readers of this book become woodburning artists? No. Which ones will? That question cannot be answered conclusively, but one thing is certain. You will never know what you can do and how involved you will want to be in woodburning until you have tried it. As your skill develops with practice and you use whatever degree of artistic talent you possess, you may even surprise yourself in the quality of the artistic woodburning you can achieve.

8-8 A study in lyrical beauty by Audronē. Plaque is part of Woodring Craft collection.

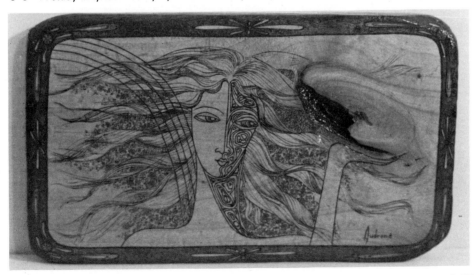

8-9   Lady with feathers by Audronē. Plaque is part of Woodring Craft collection.

8-10
8-11   Woodring Craft bracelet collection, designed and woodburned by Audronē.
8-12

SUPPLY SOURCES

Your best source of supplies is apt to be your local retail stores who stock craft and art supplies, especially those who specialize in those areas. Abrasives, white craft glue, graphite tracing paper, acrylic paints, and miscellaneous supplies will be relatively easy to buy. You may have a little more difficulty in finding a good woodburning pen and specific wood products, though almost every craft supply store stocks a large variety of plaques and so on.

If you do have problems finding a local source of supplies, the following list of companies and their addresses may be helpful. Let me caution you that many manufacturers will not sell direct to the craftsperson or artist, but almost all will answer a letter of inquiry with information about where you can buy their products in your area. A few do have mail order privileges, so it does not hurt to ask about that in your letter to them or to request their latest catalog. However, if you are simply bypassing your local retailer and seeking to buy direct from the manufacturer in an attempt to pay lower prices, you are apt to be disappointed. The cost of handling and mailing your purchase nowadays is normally added to the retail price of the product by the manufacturer and may make it more economical to buy locally if you can.

This list could be much longer than it is, but I have included only those companies who manufacture products that I have used. Do not be afraid to use other brands if your local craft supply retailer recommends a substitution.

WOODBURNING PEN

Pyrolectric pen using plug series tap
    Post Electric Company
    P.O. Drawer P
    Andover, New Jersey 07821

Woodburning pen
    Walnut Hollow
    Rt. 2
    Dodgeville, Wisconsin 53533

SPECIALTY WOOD PRODUCTS

Boxes, crates, plaques (standard and mini), shadow boxes, shelves, etc. (redwood)
    Adco Redwood, Inc.
    200 Franklin St.
    Willits, California 95490

Boxes, crates, collector's boxes, plaques, shadow box frames, dollhouse rooms, etc.
    Clauss Manufacturing
    316 North Green St.
    Melvin, Illinois 60952

Baskets, boxes (standard and mini), cabinets, collector's boxes, crates, cutouts, planters, plaques, rings, shadow box frames, shelves, specialty shapes like lamp base, etc.
    Corner Cupboard Crafts, Inc.
    93 Main St., Box 1368
    Lilburn, Georgia 30247

Air drying modeling wood, etc.
    General Grafts Corporation
    12 Burning Tree Road
    Greenwich, Connecticut 06830

Boxes (standard and mini), collector's boxes, planters, plaques (standard and mini), shadow boxes (standard and mini), shadow box frames, specialty forms, etc. (basswood)
    O. P. Crafts Co., Inc.
    425 Warren St.
    Sandusky, Ohio 44870

Clock blanks, frames, plaques, rounds, slabs, etc. (walnut)
    Walnut Hollow
    Rt. 2
    Dodgeville, Wisconsin 53533

Arte and oval frames, crescents, plaques, rings, rods, spandrels, etc. (alderwood)
    Woodring Craft
    35 W. 44th St.
    New York, New York 10036

There are many other wood product manufacturers, so look for their products at your local craft supply shop. They will also be able to supply you with a fast-drying, lacquer-type decoupage finish that will finish your woodburning projects beautifully if you cannot find the Deft or Illinois Bronze finishes that I used.

INDEX

Numbers in italics refer to pages with illustrations.